SUCCEEDING KING LEAR

SUCCEEDING KING LEAR

Literature, Exposure, and the Possibility of Politics

Emily Sun

Fordham University Press

New York   2010

Fordham University Press has no responsibility for the persistence or accuracy of URLs for external or third-party Internet websites referred to in this publication and does not guarantee that any content on such websites is, or will remain, accurate or appropriate.

Fordham University Press also publishes its books in a variety of electronic formats. Some content that appears in print may not be available in electronic books.

Library of Congress Cataloging-in-Publication Data

Sun, Emily.
    Succeeding King Lear : literature, exposure, and the possibility of politics / Emily Sun.—1st ed.
        p.   cm.
    Includes bibliographical references and index.
    ISBN 978-0-8232-3280-2 (cloth : alk. paper)—ISBN 978-0-8232-3281-9 (pbk : alk. paper)—ISBN 978-0-8232-3282-6 (ebook)   1. Shakespeare, William, 1564–1616. King Lear.   2. Shakespeare, William, 1564–1616—Influence.   3. Politics in literature.   4. Sovereignty in literature.   5. Politics and literature.   6. Wordsworth, William, 1770–1850—Criticism and interpretation.   7. Agee, James, 1909–1955—Criticism and interpretation.   8. Evans, Walker, 1903–1975—Criticism and interpretation.   I. Title.
PR2819.S86   2010
822.3′3—dc22

                                                                    2010013604

Printed in the United States of America
First paperback printing 2013

To Alice Fan-Ying Yu

Contents

Acknowledgments

I thank my teachers Shoshana Felman and Paul Fry for their warm and generous support throughout my graduate work, when I wrote my dissertation
on Keats and Flaubert, and for their encouragement in the writing of this
present book. Shoshana Felman continues to inspire me with the integrity,
courage, and power of her intellectual example, and her work never ceases
to open up for me new paths of reading and thinking. Paul Fry has enriched
my literary education immeasurably with the erudition and subtlety of his
thinking about lyric poetry, and continues to raise new interpretive possibilities for me in his writing and questioning. This book has benefited greatly
from his comments. Geoffrey Hartman's lessons retain for me, as for so
many of his students, the distinct preeminence of a renovating virtue. Bill
Pritchard's teaching and friendship have accompanied me like a treasured
gift for many years.

I thank the friends and colleagues who helped me during the writing of
this book. Eyal Peretz has been a superlatively stimulating interlocutor and
the source of crucial comments at every step of the process. Brian McGrath
read the manuscript in its entirety and gave me invaluably sensitive feed-
back. Ulrich Baer, Chimène Bateman, Elisabeth Bronfen, Ludovico Gey-
monat, Margaret Maurer, and Janet McAdams each read chapters and
provided crucial suggestions. Ulrich Baer encouraged and inspired me to
write on photography. I have enjoyed illuminating conversations about
Wordsworth with Emily Rohrbach, who invited me to present a chapter as
a talk at Hamilton College. With his typical acumen, Irad Kimhi provided
a clutch formulation at a key moment. Various colleagues in the Depart-
ment of English at Colgate University offered advice and support throughout the development of this project. I have benefited from conversations
with Susan Cerasano about *Lear*, and with Jennifer Brice about *Let Us Now
Praise Famous Men*. Lynn Staley has been all that one could wish for in a
senior colleague and mentor, and has shown me, on so many levels, the way
of the scholar. Connie Harsh and Deborah Knuth-Klenck deserve thanks

for tirelessly fielding my questions over the years and for their consistent encouragement of my work. The Colgate University Research Council offered assistance in the form of a Major Grant at an early stage of this project.

Part of chapter 4 was published as "From the Division of Labor to the Transformation of the Common: James Agee and Walker Evans's *Let Us Now Praise Famous Men*" in *Figurationen: Gender, Literatur, Kultur* 2 (2006): 33–52, in a special issue titled "The Ends of Photography," edited by Ulrich Baer.

I acknowledge Helen Tartar for her dedicated support of my work and for all her efforts in bringing this book to fruition.

I thank my friends May Chen, Maria Ting, Michael Fei, and Vera and Ava Fei for being my home away from home, my family away from family. Diti Almog has been a great pal and a genuine source of strength. Carolyn Guile has kept me in spirited company.

Finally, I thank my family. This book would not have been possible without the loving support of Edward Sun, Raymond Sun, and Alice Tsai Yu, and it is indebted to the hopes and dreams of the late Chi-Chung Yu. This book owes the most profound debt to my mother, Alice Yu—I dedicate it to her.

SUCCEEDING KING LEAR

Introduction

This book investigates Shakespeare's *King Lear* and its originative force in modern literature, with specific attention to the early work of the English Romantic poet William Wordsworth and to James Agee and Walker Evans's 1941 book *Let Us Now Praise Famous Men*. What is it about *King Lear* that makes *these*—among so many other—later readers return to the play to initiate their own creative trajectories? What is it about *King Lear* that makes these readers interrogate emphatically through the play the question of the relationship between literature and politics in modernity?

Shakespeare occupies a place of incontestable centrality in Western modernity. His work has been studied in a variety of disciplines, including—besides literary study—philosophy, history, political theory, religion, sociology, and psychology, plumbed for the insights it affords into the predicament of being modern. The empirical Shakespeare wrote toward the end of the sixteenth century and the beginning of the seventeenth, in the aftermath of the Protestant Reformation and its transformation of the institution of the English monarchy, and in the advent of the scientific revolution that would come to define the modern age.

Beyond the company of fellow English dramatists such as Jonson and Marlowe, Shakespeare has been read alongside such European thinkers as Machiavelli, Montaigne, and Descartes. The philosopher Stanley Cavell has approached the question of Shakespeare's modernity in the context of his affinity with Descartes in their common engagement with the problem of skepticism at the threshold of post-theological, scientific modernity. In another vein, the literary critic Harold Bloom claims for Shakespeare's oeuvre the status of "secular Scripture," finding the Shakespearean corpus analogous to the Bible in the intensity and magnitude of its shaping force on a wide variety of readers.[1]

This book aims to reinterpret the relations between Shakespeare and modern literary history by examining how *King Lear* generates a literary genealogy, or history of successors. Further, this book seeks to explore the

relevance of this history to the question of the relationship between literature and politics in modernity. At the heart and origin of the history *King
Lear* opens up, I argue, is a *crisis of sovereignty*. Shakespeare's plays repeatedly
interrogate sovereignty as the ontotheological principle that has traditionally
guided political life, a life that depends for its consistency and stability on an
absolute center of authority from which everything else receives its legitimacy. Modernity, it is implied, suffers a crisis in the legitimacy of this absolute source of authority. This crisis is most noticeable, for Shakespeare, at
moments of succession—when one king, the representative of absolute sovereign authority, is supposed to leave his power to a successor and enact
the orderly transfer of authority. But what Shakespeare's plays repeatedly
dramatize are events of misfire in these moments that put the principle of
sovereignty into question and expose dark areas internal to its working.

King Lear stages a crisis of sovereignty that ensues from the title character's decision to violate the indivisibility of the king's two bodies—the body
politic and the body natural—prior to his physical demise. Lear exercises
the political and legal authority, which belongs to him alone, to put himself
outside the political realm, parceling out the kingdom in exchange for
promises from his daughters to secure the freedom he thinks he will gain
thereby. In bringing to light the assumptions behind this logic, and in dramatizing its disastrous consequences, the play performs an implicit analysis and
critique of the sovereign conception of political life, particularly its relationship to freedom as represented by Lear. For Lear, freedom is an end set apart
from instead of *within* the political realm; it is conceived of as an end *outside*
of political life, which serves as means toward this end. Against this sovereign conception of freedom and political life, the play juxtaposes an alternative trajectory, enacted paradigmatically by Cordelia, in which freedom
takes place as spontaneous and unscripted action *within* instead of apart from
the political realm. It is by exposing the reader to such an event of freedom,
or to freedom as essentially political action rather than extra-political end,
that the play gestures toward the possibility of a new aesthetic and political
future beyond the disaster that it dramatizes.

This book shows how the question of the relations between literature
and politics does not only open up immanently or internally within *King
Lear*, but is also that which *opens up a history*—that which gives rise to a
succession of readers that keep returning to the play as to an originary locus
for grappling with a problem. The question of the relations between literature and politics in modernity is not resolved by *King Lear* but rather articulated in a paradigmatic manner, such that later readers return to the play in
their own attempts to deal with the question.

Among such successors, this study turns to Wordsworth in his reading play *The Borderers*, written between 1797 and 1799 and published in a revised version in 1842, as well as in the subgenre of the "encounter poem" in his corpus; and to the American writer James Agee and the photographer Walker Evans in their Depression-era book of documentary nonfiction *Let Us Now Praise Famous Men*. These texts are not adaptations or rewritings of *King Lear* in any standard sense: they do not simply copy or transpose major elements of the plot or characters of Shakespeare's tragedy to different historical or geographical contexts. Rather, they relate to fragments of the play, or to the play in fragments, enacting a practice of affiliation that complicates the traditional genealogical framework of literary historiography.

It is vitally and inescapably *as* readers of *King Lear* that Wordsworth, Agee, and Evans interrogate in their respective historical moments—the 1790s and the 1930s—the question of the relationship between literature and politics. In the 1790s, the young Wordsworth was famously grappling with the direction and destiny of his affirmation of the principle of universal humanity. In the 1930s, the young Agee and Evans encountered a level of poverty among their fellow citizens that struck them with the impoverishment of their available means of representation. At these critical moments, they turned to Shakespeare's tragedy not mournfully to express their loss of hope but to succeed *King Lear* by generating new artistic genres and modes for their times.

Sovereignty is a topic of crucial significance in the current critical scene. The philosophers Jacques Derrida and Giorgio Agamben, among others, have questioned the logic of sovereignty and interrogated its theological roots in efforts to rethink the conceptual premises of modern political thought.[2] Drawing on the work of Carl Schmitt and Michel Foucault, Agamben has argued influentially that sovereign power has traditionally constituted and stabilized itself through the production of "bare life"—or human life as if it could be, altogether unqualified and indistinguishable from plant or animal life—and the opposition of "bare life" to "form-of-life," which is life that is essentially qualified by participation in the political realm.[3] Recent theoretical efforts have been directed toward elaborating human life as always already form-of-life, essentially qualified by being-with-others, from which an element of bare life cannot be separated, as has been persistently misunderstood in the metaphysical tradition of political thought.

The present study joins such efforts, but opens up new lines of inquiry by connecting the analysis of the problem of sovereignty to the question of the literary. The history of succession traced in this book parallels and antici-pates the recent theoretical investigations: each of the literary texts in ques-tion restages both a crisis and a critique of sovereignty, and itself undertakes an interrogation of the grounds of political life. By examining how each of these texts, both by itself and in relation to one another, raises anew the question of the relationship between literature and politics, I develop an approach that revises the habitual reading of this relationship through the opposition of "text" and "context." All too often, the literary text is judged according to criteria derived from previous knowledge concerning political or historical "context"—which is implicitly given governing authority over the literary text. The specific authority of the literary text is consequently silenced or denied, and what politics *is*, moreover, remains stabilized *as* given "context" instead of being opened up, through the mutual implica-tion of the literary and the political, to further questioning.

I approach the literary texts in question not so much as texts that are *about* politics, representations of *this* or *that* past or existing "political reality," but as events that open up the possibility of politics, of democracy as irreducible to community stabilized according to given predicates or representable con-ditions of membership. The event of Cordelia's "nothing" in *King Lear* alle-gorizes poetry's power to make *nothing* happen—"nothing" precisely as event that, interrupting the givenness of who one is and how one belongs, opens up a space of creativity.

While I try to respond in my readings to the specificity of each text and to analyze how each text stages a crisis of sovereignty, I reflect further on the status and function of literature or the literary in relation to political thought as extra- or nonliterary discourse. The literary, in my readings, is that which exposes the inconsistency within political thought, its lack of sovereignty, the impossibility of political thought *as* discourse of mastery about politics to totalize itself. It is the literary that par excellence exposes the impossibility of such mastery and renews through such exposure the very possibility of politics as free, plural, and non-sovereign action.

~~~

By locating a crisis of sovereignty at the origin of the history *King Lear* opens up, this book demonstrates that one approach to thinking about literary his-tory is through the model of traumatic repetition. History opens up pre-cisely when there is something too overwhelming for the understanding, such as the crisis of sovereignty, which generates a pattern of compulsive return as to a primal traumatic moment. *King Lear* both stages such a crisis of sovereignty in the content of the play as well as constitutes for its readers as play itself *the event of crisis*. It occasions readers to return to work through the question of the relations between literature and politics that the play shows paradigmatically but does not resolve.

My reading of literary history through the model of traumatic repetition differs from the standard humanist approach to literary history. It also deviates from such an influential model as Harold Bloom's, based on his theory of the anxiety of influence, according to which each generation of writers participates in an Oedipal struggle to replace the paternal authority of previous generations. If, in the Bloomian model, the question of authority or sovereignty is likewise at stake, authority or sovereignty defines precisely that which is to be gained by the next generation of writers. In my approach, sovereignty is not what is to be gained but precisely that which is in crisis in literary history, from whose logic writers try to free themselves rather than seek to perpetuate, as in Bloom.[4] In this way, I bring writers of British Romanticism and American Modernism in touch with their literary political origins in Shakespeare.

I investigate how Wordsworth returns to Shakespeare at the beginning of his career in the 1790s, prior to his well-known return to Milton, to articulate and invent a new kind of literature that would liberate humanity from the imperatives of sovereignty at the dawn of a new democratic age. The young Wordsworth greeted the beginning of an era that saw the transfer of sovereignty from monarchs to "the people," the *demos* of democracy, when every human being qua citizen of a democratic nation-state is supposed to be at once in relation to his fellows both sovereign and subject, ruler and ruled. He and others of his generation embraced this new sense of fellowship founded on the principle of equality between all human beings as rational animals, capable as users of reason of legislating themselves without recourse to divine authority, and no longer differentiated according to the received criteria of birth, blood, or inherited rank. Based on his experience as eyewitness and actor in the French Revolution, Wordsworth found reason alone, however, insufficient as a basis for community. He sought instead, through the medium of poetry, to create or articulate a "common ground," or the "common" as ground.

"Nature" is his figure for this common ground, the basis for the "common language" or the language of "man speaking to men" he claims for poetry in his 1800 Preface to *Lyrical Ballads*. But Wordsworth's treatment of nature splits into nature, on the one hand, as the sacralized *outside* of the political realm become means to freedom as end; and, on the other hand, nature as the uncanny event of "nothing" that traverses discourse and takes place within the political sphere, for which there is no outside, in which human life is always already form-of-life, "citizen" congruent with and inseparable from "man."

In the first instance, nature as sacralized "outside" serves as site of not just freedom from the political realm but of a symmetrical exposure outside of politics, an abandonment of human life as naked or bare life that confirms the sovereign structure of the nation-state as well as the sovereign authority of the poet. In the second case, nature is an a-topic topos through which the poet registers another kind of exposure—his exposure to the unassimilable alterity of the others he encounters, an exposure that marks his lack of sovereignty over his own speech and story as well as over the speech and stories of others.

In the autobiographical turn he introduces into his poetry of the "common," Wordsworth registers in his own experience and brings to perceptibility the events of "nothing" that mark his encounters with others and that hauntingly inhabit his memory and consciousness. In *The Borderers*, a threshold work of his oeuvre, Wordsworth returns to the heath in *King Lear* to convert it into an a-topic topos, the site of a readerly exposure to the unassimilable alterity of others, instead of the site of an exposure or abandonment outside of political space altogether. It is on "nature" as a-topic topos, I claim, that Wordsworth founds his poetry of the common.

As the most significant and at the same time most elusive term in Wordsworth's poetry, "nature" cannot in its instability be simply understood as another instantiation of the nature/culture dichotomy (e.g., a Rousseauist "state of nature" vs. a Burkean "second nature" of customs, habits, affections, and inherited practices).[5] Rather, "nature" as a-topic topos operates beyond these two as force or event to unsettle their opposition. It is in the unsettling effect of "nature" in this latter sense that I locate Wordsworth's originality and his development of a new logic of the literary.

If in his poetic practice Wordsworth transformatively extends "the common"—rather than merely confirming "the common" as already known and "the common man" as if it corresponded to a given identity—so too do Agee and Evans in their creation of an altogether-unprecedented mode of communication in *Let Us Now Praise Famous Men*. Commissioned by *Fortune* magazine to report on the situation of cotton tenant farmers in the American Deep South during the Depression, they refused to perform the assignment as such, to represent those they were reporting about simply as tenant farmers from the perspective of themselves in their occupational articulation as journalists. In reinventing their task, they unwork the prevailing political economic conception of society in terms of the division of labor.

At the beginning of his text, Agee establishes parallels between his and Evans's predicaments in Alabama in 1936 and those of Lear on the heath and Edgar in his internal exile in the kingdom. He finds himself and Evans in a situation of abandonment or exposure symmetrical to that of the tenant farmers viewed as outcasts or "poor naked wretches." If the latter appear to be excluded from participating in a society of mutually shared interests, Agee and Evans find themselves likewise estranged from a reading and viewing public in which they are supposed to have a vested stake. Working in their respective media, they launch an aesthetic experiment that aims to open up a new understanding of what it is, au fond, to participate and have a stake in the common. Evans, in his photographs, does not just show his subjects as objects to the viewer but tries to show how his subjects see—that is, he *exposes to the viewer his seeing of another's seeing*. Agee, in his text, moves between a heterogeneity of allusions, genres, modes, and styles to disclose to the reader the shame he feels in being exposed to the unassimilable shame of the other, who is, equally yet incommensurably, like him actor and spectator in the world among others.

The figure of theater guides and informs my readings of all the texts in question, be they in the genre of drama or lyric poetry, autobiography, documentary nonfiction, or photography. Theater is the political art par excellence, in that it both shows and takes place in the world as a space of appearances, in which human beings live essentially in the plural among one another and speak and interact with one another to administer the affairs they have in common. Hannah Arendt situates political life as a life of action in the world as a space of appearances, in relation to which the solitary life of the mind, and its corollary contemptus mundi, must be thought—no longer, however, in terms of a hierarchical opposition of thought's privilege over action, as in the Platonic-Cartesian metaphysical tradition, but from within the world as a space of appearances that cannot be stabilized and viewed from a God-like perspective (i.e., from the outside).[6] The Oedipal legacy of tragic heroism is characterized by the tendency to try to master one's own destiny by adopting in relation to it this sovereign, God-like perspective, according to which freedom is secured and affirmed in denial of the inherently unpredictable character of action. *King Lear* is a tragedy that powerfully gestures toward the possibility of going beyond this dominant tragic mode to open up a new logic of literary succession.

I. *Shakespeare*

1.   *Sovereignty, Exposure, Theater*

A Reading of *King Lear*

> No man can be sovereign because not one man, but men, inhabit the earth.
>
>   HANNAH ARENDT, *The Human Condition*

What are the political stakes of reading or watching a play? How might a literary work, specifically a work of theater, shed light on our human existence as essentially plural political beings? I propose to examine in this chapter how Shakespeare's *King Lear* itself raises these questions. The tragedy stages a radical interrogation of what it is to be a reader or spectator in relation to others in the political realm. Through its unrelenting and cruel probing of spectatorship, I contend, *King Lear* exposes us, beyond sovereignty, to the possibility of an aesthetics and politics of plurality.

King Lear *between Past and Future*

The plot of *King Lear* is well-known. The play begins with the protagonist's extraordinary announcement that he will give up the throne and divide his kingdom between his three daughters. For each third of the kingdom each daughter is requested to declare her love for her father in public. His two older daughters comply, while the youngest, Cordelia, would rather keep silent and say "nothing" than speak her love this way. In response to Cordelia's defiance, Lear banishes her as well as his loyal courtier, Kent, who has dared to contest his decision. Lear moves with his retinue to the house first of his oldest daughter, Goneril, then her sister Regan, finding belatedly that he no longer enjoys the position of authority he had effectively given up. Leaving Regan's house on the brink of a storm, Lear and his followers find themselves exposed to the elements on the heath. There Lear loses his wits, and only regains his sanity after reencountering his courtier Gloucester, who has in the meantime been blinded; and after reconciling with Cordelia, who, now Queen of France, has returned to Britain at the head of an army to save her father from her sisters, who first schemed together, then against each other, in bids for power.

Intertwined with this plot is a subplot involving Gloucester and his sons. Gloucester's bastard son, Edmund, dupes his father into believing that his half brother, Edgar, is plotting to kill him, and Edmund thereby usurps Edgar's position as legitimate heir. Edmund then allies himself with Goneril and Regan against his own father, who is blinded at the hands of Regan and her husband, Cornwall. Edgar has in the meantime gone into internal exile in the kingdom by adopting a series of disguises. He comes across Lear and his own father while in disguise but does not reveal who he is, plotting to clear his name and take revenge by fighting his brother. The plot and the subplot converge in the final scene on a battlefield in the vicinity of Dover. Edgar defeats Edmund in a duel. Goneril and Regan kill each other over their mutual paramour, Edmund. Then Lear returns carrying the dead body of Cordelia. The pair had been captured by enemy forces, and Cordelia hanged according to Edmund's orders. Lear dies of suffocation over Cordelia's dead body. The play ends with the three surviving characters— Goneril's husband, Albany; Kent; and Edgar—speaking of how to sustain "the gored state." Putatively, at the end, Edgar emerges as the survivor-king.

The plot of *King Lear* was well-known already to Shakespeare. Writing the play sometime after 1603, between *Othello* and *Macbeth*, Shakespeare drew on accounts of a historical Lear with three daughters who reigned in Britain around 800 B.C.E. These accounts were available in folk sources and in the *Chronicles* of Holinshed, which were probably also the sources for a contemporary play published anonymously in 1605, *The True Chronicle Historie of King Leir*. The subplot involving Gloucester and his sons Shakespeare may have derived from a passage in book II of Sidney's *Arcadia*.[1] The result of this collage and adaptation of extant material was a play that, according to the title page of the 1608 Quarto, had its first performance before James I "at Whitehall upon S. Stephans night in Christmas Hollidayes"—December 26, 1606—by "his Majesties servants playing usually at the Gloabe on the Bancke-side."[2]

His use of Holinshed suggests that Shakespeare may have been extending in *Lear* the study of kingship—the Plantagenets, in particular—that he had undertaken in the history plays, from the early *Henry VI* works to, most recently, *Henry V*. Notably, apart from the histories, *Macbeth* is the only other play for which Shakespeare consulted Holinshed. In the history plays, Shakespeare revisits the history of Britain as by definition a succession of sovereigns, but he does more, of course, than simply adopt and transpose Holinshed's perspective for drama. The plays illuminate in complex ways the conflicts internal to the principle of kingship itself, conflicts most obviously externalized in the murders and usurpations that, paradoxically, derail at the same time as they sustain dynastic succession. These external conflicts repeat the cyclical contest to answer the question, who has the right to rule? The answer to this question remains predictable: the king. Underlying the cycle of internecine violence is the principle that whoever bears the title of king exercises the right to govern. The history plays investigate repeatedly in the medium of theater the instability inherent in the notion of a divinely mandated kingship at the core of the tradition of political theology.[3]

In *Lear* Shakespeare explores the vexed nature of kingship by turning to a mythical king in the distant past, a "prehistoric" figure whose doings predate the practice of historical record keeping. He makes no mention in the play of any predecessor kings, nor specifically names Lear's queen, and leaves ambiguous the question of succession. Lear is an old man— "fourscore and upwards," we learn late in the play—who has ruled for a long time, so long that none of the other characters ever recall a period before Lear's rule. Shakespeare does not situate the play in a dynastic context in which the action of the tragedy would constitute, as it were, an episodic excerpt. Instead, the action of the tragedy seems strangely abstracted out of the continuum of historical time. *Lear* is a *legendary* play, both in the sense of its being based on ancient, fragmentarily available material and its functioning, according to the etymology of the word "legend," as that through which kingship itself is to be interpreted allegorically.

If Shakespeare, at the advent of modernity, turns to the distant past to offer a reading of kingship, how has this reading in turn been read by the future (i.e., the future that is our past)? To begin with, I would like to mention that even within the notoriously unstable Shakespearean corpus, *King Lear* is distinguished by having the most fragile textual history. The divisions of the text parallel the division of the kingdom.[4] The first textual division to present itself is that between the versions of the play in the 1608 Quarto and the 1623 First Folio. The 1608 version purports to be based on the script used for the play's performance at Whitehall on Saint Stephen's Night, 1606, while the 1623 Folio was the one edited by Shakespeare's fellow actors to serve as the standard reading text. More than with other Shakespeare plays, these versions feature different passages and different line attributions.[5] Editors today typically amalgamate the two versions. It is the imperfect Arden edition that I use.[6]

To further complicate matters, a division of another order emerged— between the reading text and the acting text—when Nahum Tate reworked the play during the Restoration, eliminating the Fool and giving the story a happy ending, with the marriage of Cordelia and Edgar. Between 1681 and 1838 the Tate version served as the text for all stage representations. The eighteenth century thus saw a curious split between the reading text of *King Lear* and the Tate acting text. Even Samuel Johnson in his 1765 note on *King Lear* would claim to prefer the Tate version because he was unable to bear the horror of Cordelia's death: "I was many years ago so shocked by Cordelia's death, that I know not whether I ever endured to read again the last scenes of the play till I undertook to revise them as an editor."[7] For Johnson, it took the palliative of editorial perspective to mitigate the traumatic experience of reading the play.

A striking turn in the reception of *King Lear* occurred in the middle of the twentieth century, when the tragedy replaced *Hamlet* as the most highly regarded and frequently performed of Shakespeare's plays, as R. A. Foakes has documented.[8] It seems that *King Lear* emerged in the 1950s as the play that had the most to teach audiences living in the aftermath of the genocidal horror and global total warfare of the Second World War and the development of nuclear weapons capable of annihilating the world. In the second half of the twentieth century, the tragedy inspired various adaptations and rewritings, including Beckett's *Endgame*, Edward Bond's *Lear*, and Kurosawa's *Ran*. Further, it has been the subject of scores of critical interpretations. Shakespeare's *King Lear* has entered the fabric of artistic and critical discourse as a play somehow capable of shedding light on catastrophe, of providing illumination in the wake—and in the midst—of disaster.

The Task of the Spectator

> How can one speak so that speech is essentially plural?
>
> Maurice Blanchot, *The Infinit*

At the very end of the play, one of the surviving characters—the Quarto, and Edgar in the Folio—remarks:

> The weight of this sad time we must obey,
> Speak what we feel, not what we ought to say.
> The oldest hath borne most; we that are young
> Shall never see so much, nor live so long.

(5.

These lines may be said to constitute the first reading of the play—a p nary attempt at formulating the question of what it is to have seen *Kir*

To have seen *King Lear*, the closing couplet suggests, is never to s same way again. It is to undergo an alienation of seeing wherein the y are differentiated from the old, one generation from another. What ren ambiguous is whether the young feel respectfully mournful in relatio this older way of seeing or whether the couplet merely indicates, with further affective determination, that a rupture in seeing has taken place. F ther, the quatrain establishes a link between the break in seeing and t change in speaking called for in the second line. Apposite with the break seeing is the emergence of an imperative to "speak what we feel, not wh: we ought to say."

This chapter will dedicate itself to examining the structure of this break in seeing and its relationship to an altered speech. Suffice it to say prelimi-narily that the task of the spectator—which is the task of succeeding *King Lear*—is *not* to repeat again what has happened in the play, but to make a new beginning that breaks with the cycle of tragic repetition.

Before proceeding, I turn briefly to a previous reading of guiding impor-tance to my own: the philosopher Stanley Cavell's classic essay "The Avoid-ance of Love," published in 1969 and the inaugural essay in a series of reflections on Shakespeare and themes Shakespearean.[9] Cavell draws atten-tion to the then current interpretive debate over the so-called sight pattern of the play—salient imagery having to do with seeing and the uses of eyes. Differing with Paul Alpers and other Shakespeare scholars, Cavell observes that "the isolation and avoidance of eyes is what the obsessive sight imagery of the play underlines": eyes are emphasized in the play *not* in the characters' capacity for seeing but in their avoidance of being seen.[10] For example, Cornwall blinds Gloucester so that Gloucester cannot see Cornwall's evil deeds. Cavell locates at the heart of this sight imagery "the same motivation which manipulates the tragedy throughout its course, from the scene which precedes the abdication, through the storm, blinding, evaded reconciliations, to the final moments: the attempt to avoid recognition, the shame of exposure, the threat of self-revelation."[11] The characters avoid, deny, banish, and fail to recognize others because they do not allow themselves to be recognized. Lear's recognition of Gloucester and Cordelia can take place only when he allows himself to be recognized.

The attention Cavell devotes to scenes of recognition in the play implicitly revises the traditional understanding of this key term in the history and structure of tragedy. In the *Poetics*, Aristotle defines anagnorisis on a basic level as "a change from ignorance to knowledge," referring for a paradigmatic instance to Oedipus's discovery of his identity from the Corinthian messenger.[12] In the classic understanding, recognition takes a character from ignorance to knowledge—figuratively, from blindness to seeing. Oedipus had, figuratively, been "blind" to his own identity previously, but now he "sees" who he is; but now that he "sees" who he is, he blinds himself literally. Seeing as a figure of knowledge in this instance is construed as denial of the world of appearances or sensory perception, over which Oedipus had been deceived in previously thinking himself master, but over which, paradoxically, he reestablishes himself as master by disavowing completely.

Cavell's analysis of recognition in *King Lear* swerves from the Aristotelian-Oedipal model and replaces the terms "ignorance" and "knowledge," and the implied linear progression from one to the other, with the terms "avoidance" and "acknowledgment," with something more like an oscillatory movement between them. Tragic recognition in *Lear*, according to Cavell's analysis, involves a displacement of the epistemological categories traditionally privileged by Aristotelian poetics.

Following Cavell's reading, I unravel further how the play sheds light on what it is to see and to be seen, and to relate to others as spectator or reader in the political realm. These questions apply to the characters in the play as well as to the reader or audience of the play.

But, first of all, let us specify that the political realm in question is a kingdom, and the characters in question members of this kingdom that the king jolts, in the very first scene, into an exceptional situation. To this kingdom out of joint let us now turn.

Theater at the Limit of Sovereignty

> If it is said that the theater came forth from the realm of ritual, what is meant
> is that it became theater when it left that realm.
>
> Bertolt Brecht, *A Little Organon for the Theater*

The play shows in its first scene the king staging and performing his last act as king. Lear takes the extraordinary step of doing what only he has the political and legal authority to do: namely, exercise the power to end his power. He abdicates and divides the kingdom because, as he declares to the assembled court, "'tis our fast intent/To shake all cares and business from our age,/Conferring them on younger strengths, while we/Unburdened crawl toward death" (1.1.37–40). He claims to arrange this so "that future strife/May be prevented now" (1.1.43–4), unwittingly paving the way precisely for future strife. After abdicating, Lear plans to take turns staying with his daughters, "[w]ith reservation of an hundred knights/By you to be sustained" (1.1.134–5). Investing his daughters with his "power,/Pre-eminence and all the large effects/That troop with majesty," he expects he can still "retain/The name, and all th'addition to a king" (1.1.131–3, 136–7). To say the least, things do not work according to plan for him. When his plan starts to go awry, he mentions also that, as part of his envisioned future, he had "thought to set my rest/On [Cordelia's] kind nursery" (1.1.123–4).

By giving up power and dividing the kingdom, Lear enters into an extraordinary and precarious situation. He becomes, in effect, a man who has no title or part in the political realm. Kenneth Burke has framed this problem in terms of what he calls the "paradox of substance"—"substance" being a word that has come to designate "what a thing *is*" while deriving etymologically from "a word designating something that a thing *is not*."[13] "What is a king without a kingdom," Burke asks apropos Lear before continuing, "a sea captain without a ship, a general without an army, a politician out of office, a jobholder without his job?"[14]

In a related vein, Jacques Lacan sheds light on Lear's predicament in *The Ethics of Psychoanalysis*, mentioning Lear after Oedipus and Antigone as a modern tragic figure who enters the zone between two deaths, "l'entre-deux-morts"—between death as withdrawal from the network of symbolic reality, and real or biological death.[15] To this space had Oedipus come at the end of *Oedipus the King* and in *Oedipus at Colonus*, and Antigone when she refuses Creon's authority and thereby excludes herself from the community.[16] Lear too crosses over into this exceptional zone.

"So,/When I am nothing—then am I a man?," asks Oedipus in *Oedipus at Colonus*.[17] Shakespeare's *King Lear*, I claim, repeats this question, beginning when the king ceases to be king and becomes, instead, a man without title or part in the kingdom. It treats in complex ways the question of what it is to be a human being precisely *as* the question of what it is to be without title or part in the kingdom.[18]

The problem is that Lear misunderstands this predicament. To unpack this misunderstanding, I pursue a remark by Lacan in his brief comments on the play in *The Ethics of Psychoanalysis*—namely, that Lear seems to picture his entry into the zone between two deaths as "the beginning of freedom, a life of festivities with his knights, lots of fun, during which time he stays in turn with each of those two shrews whom he thought he could entrust with the duties of power."[19] At stake in Lear's plans for life after abdication is a certain conception of *freedom*. To be a man without a role in the kingdom is, for Lear, to begin a life of freedom. Let us consider more closely the structure of his envisioned freedom.

Lear's conception of freedom involves being disburdened of the duties of state, which he hands over to his daughters. Having no role or part, he would enjoy instead a supra-role situated above or outside the political realm.[20] (Fittingly, the map Lear uses in the first scene as a prop for the division of the kingdom illustrates the political realm as a finite whole that can be partitioned into parts without remainder.) Lear anticipates enjoying, at last, at the end of his living years, a freedom that has been deferred during the years of government. Significantly, freedom so conceived is set apart from instead of *within* the political realm; it is conceived of as an end *outside* of political life, which serves as a means toward this end. Freedom so conceived does not take place *between* men, in a realm of human affairs where human beings speak and act with each other to decide the affairs and interests they have in common. Rather, topologically opposed to the political realm, freedom so conceived simulates the freedom enjoyed by God or gods—as evinced in the captured Lear's enraptured comparison of himself and Cordelia in act 5 to "God's spies," an ironic confusion of captivity with freedom.

According to this topology, the political realm must appear, from the perspective of freedom, as a whole *outside* of which freedom can take place. For

Lear to enjoy freedom as a man without title or part in the political realm, the political realm must appear to him precisely as an organized totality in which subjects have titles and parts. It is to stabilize the political realm for the sake of his freedom that Lear attaches to his decision to abdicate and divide the kingdom the stipulation that his daughters declare their love for him: "Which of you shall we say doth love us most,/That we our largest bounty may extend/Where nature doth with merit challenge" (1.1.51–3).

Lear tries to secure his freedom, as Lacan remarks, "with no other warrant than that of loyalty, of an agreement founded on honor" (305). What he wants from his daughters is not love but *promises*, which he mistakenly equates with love: in effect, what he wants from each of them is her word that she will play the part necessary for the kingdom to be organized in such a way that he can have his freedom.

Before the court has assembled and before he asks his daughters to profess their love, Lear has already made up his mind to give up the throne and divide the kingdom into thirds. The contest implied in his request— "Which of you shall we say doth love us most/That we our largest bounty may extend"—is actually spurious because Lear has already determined which third to give each daughter. No matter how she speaks, each daughter will receive her portion of land—none larger than the other, with Cordelia's the "most opulent"—provided that she declare her love in superlative terms. Grammatically, his request is not really a question but a command whose answer he has determined in advance, as he has in turn already determined his own response to the answer. Asking a genuine question of another implies, of course, not already knowing the other's answer and thus ceding initiative to the other, who retains the capacity to surprise the questioner. Lear's request in the form of a command denies the possibility of surprise. Thinking that he is asking for love, Lear demands rather declarations that would validate the decision he has already made, speeches that would have the force of countersignatures to the contract he has drawn up. Contrary to many interpretations, Lear is not trying to buy love with land; he is, first of all, trying to buy freedom with land, a bargain that includes freedom *from love*.

Goneril and Regan agree to play their designated parts, auditioning with gusto for the eyes and ears of their father, competing to appear to the king and the entire court the way they think he wants them to appear. One claims to love him in a way that exceeds language and all measure, the other claims that she is "alone felicitate/In your dear highness's love." Their performances imply their total agreement with his *will*—both in the sense of the word as volition and as testamentary document; their performances give assent to the decision he has already made, maintaining continuity between the sovereign's sentences and his power. To reward them for their performances, Lear gives them their allotted shares: to Goneril, "all these bounds, even from this line to this,/With shadowy forests and with champaigns riched,/With plenteous rivers and wide-skirted meads" (1.1.63–5); and to Regan, "this ample third of our fair kingdom,/No less in space, validity and pleasure/Than that conferred on Goneril" (1.1.80–2). The trouble for Lear comes, of course, when his youngest daughter refuses to play the part she is asked to play.

When it is Cordelia's turn to speak, she says "nothing." Pressed by Lear to speak again, she says, "I cannot heave/My heart into my mouth. I love your majesty/According to my bond, no more nor less" (1.1.91–3). And when pressed to "mend her speech," she explains in her own defense:

> Good my lord,
> You have begot me, bred me, loved me. I
> Return those duties back as are right fit,
> Obey you, love you and most honour you.
> Why have my sisters husbands, if they say
> They love you all? Haply when I shall wed,
> That lord whose hand must take my plight shall carry
> Half my love with him, half my care and duty.
> Sure I shall never marry like my sisters
> To love my father all.
>
> (1.1.95–104)

A common complaint is that Cordelia sounds here curiously priggish, coldly calculating and parsimonious in the way she metes and doles out love. The speech is indeed somewhat baffling, so let us consider it more carefully.

What Cordelia is arguing is that it is logically impossible for her to love her father *all*, and that her sisters are committing a logical fallacy when they make that claim. The decision of her marriage is the next item on Lear's agenda, and if she is to be married she will, like her sisters, have two lords, not just one, and would thus be unable to love her father all. She points out that she will have the obligation of playing the part of a wife in addition to the part of a daughter. She will have more than one role to play and cannot thus play the part of loving above all and only Lear. She will have to move between multiple lords and play multiple roles instead of assuming *the* role

Lear wants her to play in the political realm as a totality of parts that guarantees his end of freedom.

But the play goes further and shows a more fundamental split in the way Cordelia speaks of love beyond her argument concerning the rationalization of roles. In two asides to the audience after each of her sisters' performances, Cordelia speaks of love in another way:

> What shall Cordelia speak? Love, and be silent.
>
> (1.1.62)

>   I am sure my love's
> More ponderous than my tongue.
>
> (1.1.77–8)

These asides are, by definition, remarks that Lear and the rest of the court do not hear. The love Cordelia speaks of in these asides is hidden from the world and resists appearing between men as something available to sensory perception. The play thus registers a split or division within speech when it comes to love. "Nothing" is the word that marks this split: "nothing" interrupts the speaking of love and divides it into what cannot be expressed before others and what can be said but only in measured terms.

By saying "nothing," Cordelia refuses to perform the role Lear wants her to play and rejects the theatrical contract he wants his daughters to validate in staging his last act as king. She does not give him the speech he demands, which is the promise that she will play her part in securing the political realm for his freedom. Instead, she explains to him, according to the very logic that envisions the political realm as a totality of parts, that she cannot play only that part but must assume multiple roles, fulfill multiple duties and bonds.

But that is not all. Cordelia does not simply say that she will participate in more than one sovereign totality and be subject to more than one lord, as if she would simply be moving between a plurality of like totalities—from Britain to France or Burgundy—in which she would be subordinate in each as princess or queen. The "nothing" that she speaks insists on something radically in excess of *any* political realm defined as such, an excess that keeps *any* kingdom from closing in on and completing itself as a whole in which one is subjected as a member who has title and part. "Nothing" disturbs the sovereignty of the political realm and unsettles at the same time its function as principle that governs in turn the relationship between realms. "Nothing" exposes the limit of sovereignty.

But, paradoxically, it is precisely by saying "nothing" that Cordelia makes her love perceptible in court—a space dominated now by its function as site of juridical-political decision (i.e., as courtroom). "Nothing" makes love perceptible in court precisely as a silence or caesura.[21] In "nothing," the play shows Cordelia's love for Lear as precisely a love for him as *whatever*, exposing the gap that keeps love for another from being collapsed with loving another as father, husband, king, or lord, a role in relation to which one would know and play the adequate or commensurate part.[22] To love someone as *whatever* implies that this someone is singular and unexchangeable, irreducible to attributes and qualities that can be shared with others, while to love someone as king, father, daughter, or heir—the bearer of a title or part that in turn determines one's own title or part—denies the other's specific uniqueness as it does one's own uniqueness. The latter implicitly defines someone according to qualities that make this someone like or unlike others—a type or "character," with all the theatrical connotations of the terms.

Bearing the title and playing the part of king, Lear's specific uniqueness is already given, articulated in advance by the hierarchical organization of the kingdom. He is one; there is none other like him. By abdicating and dividing the kingdom, he thinks he is making a free and sovereign decision to begin enjoying his freedom, but he is unaware of the division his decision opens up. Who he is will no longer be identical to his title and role, the supreme title and role to which all other titles and roles in the kingdom refer. Instead of enjoying, as he envisions, a supra-role in relation to the political realm, Lear must embark on the process of discovering who he is as a man without title or role in the kingdom.

Cordelia's "nothing" exposes Lear as without title or role at the same time as it exposes his being loved *as* being irreducible to having a title or role. Lear finds this "nothing" unbearable: it invalidates the theatrical contract he has drafted to secure his freedom. In saying "nothing," Cordelia performs an act that departs from the paternal script, disrupting the circuit wherein her identity would be confirmed by virtue of her reciprocation of the sovereign gaze. In exceeding type or character as dictated by Lear's theater of sovereignty, she is a character who shows "character" instead in another sense—insofar as the term designates not just a nominal object but the action or process of disclosing one's specific uniqueness. Showing character beyond character, Cordelia performs an act beyond the act. Acting in excess of title and role to acknowledge the loved one in his being without title and role, Cordelia performs precisely a *free act*.

The play brings into appearance thereby an event of freedom structurally alternative to Lear's, which opposes freedom as end to the political realm as means toward this end. He who makes a free qua sovereign decision stands over and against this realm as transcendent judge; the members of the kingdom sustain this sovereign freedom as title-bearing subjects who play designated parts. The political realm appears as a totality available to being *known*. Cordelia's "nothing," on the other hand, introduces freedom *into* the political realm as an action or event that takes place between human actors, in which what the actor is cannot be reduced to type or character and remains radically *unknown* while the singularity of who she is gets disclosed. If in Lear's conception of freedom we find the classical privileging in Western thought of knowledge over action, Cordelia's enactment of freedom unsettles this hierarchy.[23]

"Nothing" sets into motion the protagonist's and the play's departure from the closed realm of ritual into the uncertain world of theater. Unhinging Lear's ritualistic theater of sovereignty, "nothing" throws the kingdom out of joint. The theater that is *King Lear* emerges precisely from this dislocation of the framework of sovereignty. Time itself is thrown out of joint insofar as time is understood in terms of the framework of a history of predictable sovereign succession. As agent of this dislocation, the signifier "nothing" will reverberate as leitmotif throughout the language of the play in the mouths of various characters.[24] Its initial iteration generates already a sequence of echoes:

LEAR   Speak.
CORDELIA   Nothing, my lord.
LEAR   Nothing?
CORDELIA   Nothing.
LEAR   How, nothing will come of nothing. Speak again.

(1.1.86–90)

To this "nothing" Lear responds with the instrument of banishment. He disowns Cordelia immediately by swearing by "the sacred radiance of the sun, / The mysteries of Hecate and the night, / By all the operation of the orbs / From whom we do exist and cease to be" (1.1.110–3). "Hence and avoid my sight," he orders her, "So be my grave my peace, as here I give / Her father's heart from her" (1.1.124–5). He then banishes Kent, who has dared to contest his decision and intercede on Cordelia's behalf: "Out of my sight!" Lear cries, giving him six days to "turn thy hated back / Upon our kingdom" (1.1.176–7). Lear excludes Cordelia and Kent completely from the kingdom, ex-posing them by placing them *outside* the kingdom altogether to stabilize the political realm for his freedom. Topologically, then, freedom and banishment appear as symmetrical opposites of each other in relation to the political realm as sovereign totality. Through banishment Lear thinks he has thereby preserved his freedom.

Banishment is the juridical-political action repeated throughout the play to preserve or establish sovereignty. After Cordelia and Kent, Edgar, Gloucester, the Fool, and Lear himself will suffer the predicament of banishment or exile from the kingdom. Just as Lear banishes Cordelia and Kent, Gloucester banishes Edgar; Lear, Kent, and the Fool find themselves banished by Regan and Goneril; and Cornwall and Regan banish Gloucester. The banished become, from the perspective of the claim to sovereignty, those deprived of title or part, whose exclusion paradoxically confirms the very logic of sovereignty. The play opens up for discovery, however, beyond freedom and banishment in an extra-political sense, an alternative conception of what it is to be human precisely in terms of what it is not to have title or part in the kingdom. Right at the beginning of the play, the event of Cordelia's "nothing" introduces the very possibility of this alternative.

The Plot That Follows the Plot

Let us turn now to the following scene. In a peripheral household, another drama begins. The play moves in act 1, scene 2 from Lear's court, the top and center of the political hierarchy, to the subordinate household of Gloucester, where a successive and parallel crisis breaks out between a father and his children that results similarly in the banishment of a child. Commonly termed in Shakespeare scholarship the "subplot" of the tragedy, the drama of Gloucester's family derives from an entirely different source than the material Shakespeare used for the story of Lear and his daughters. By interweaving plot and subplot, Shakespeare brings together two separate but elliptically related crises of succession that shed light on each other, subtended as they are by principles that regulate center and periphery alike.

I approach the Gloucester subplot as one that effectively *follows* the Lear plot in several senses. Most obviously, the subplot comes after the Lear plot in the chronological unfolding of the play. Gloucester's family comes after Lear's in terms of the political organization of the kingdom. As member of Lear's court, Gloucester is by definition a follower of Lear as leader. Gloucester follows Lear also to the extent that his understanding of himself as father and head of his own household is oriented by and modeled after the king as father and head of state. But perhaps the most obvious point remains the most significant one, for what takes place in Gloucester's household could not have taken place, I intend to show, without Gloucester's having been a spectator in Lear's court in the opening scene.

It is in utter disorientation that Gloucester returns from Lear's court to his own home. Upon entering, he puzzles, "Kent banished thus? and France in choler parted?/And the King gone tonight? Prescribed his power,/Confined to exhibition? All this done/Upon the gad?" (1.2.23–6). "These late eclipses in the sun and moon/portend no good to us," he tries to explain a little later. "Love cools, friendship/falls off, brothers divide: in cities, mutinies; in/countries, discord; in palaces, treason; and the bond/cracked 'twixt son and father" (1.2.103–4, 106–9). It is this disorientation that renders him peculiarly susceptible to Edmund's deception—a gullibility that has long baffled commentators on the play. It is Gloucester's having been part of Lear's audience that makes for the elliptical repetition in his own household of what he had seen and heard in another scene.

Through the subplot the tragedy begins, then, to follow its own plot and thereby to allegorize the effects of its own viewing. The principals of the subplot consist of Gloucester; his older and legitimate son, Edgar; and the bastard, Edmund. At various points each of these characters performs some kind of spectatorial function in relation to the development of the play. Gloucester is introduced at the very beginning specifically in his capacity as spectator, trading remarks with Kent, like two seasoned theatergoers, about the scene they are about to see—

KENT   I thought the King had more affected the Duke of
Albany than Cornwall.
GLOUCESTER   It did always seem so to us: but now, in the
division of the kingdom, it appears not which of the
dukes he values most . . . .

(1.1.1–5)

—and he returns home as a viewer whose expectations have been foiled.

Both Edgar and Edmund also assume significant meta-theatrical functions at different points of the play. Between them the brothers speak the bulk of the asides and soliloquies in *King Lear*. In the second half, Edgar emerges as the play's privileged spectator, commenting through various disguises on developments of the plot, on other characters, and on his reactions to them. In the first half, Edmund resembles a playwright or director who reveals to the audience in soliloquies and asides how he will manipulate his father and brother as actors in the plot of usurpation he has devised.

I propose, then, to investigate how the principal actors of the subplot follow and perform spectatorial functions in relation to the Lear plot, and I hypothesize, moreover, that this following of the Lear plot as, implicitly, "master plot" structures and deforms these characters' relationships with one another.

Let us turn first to Edmund, the bastard, who, from his paradoxical position as outsider within the kingdom, puts the subplot into motion. He reveals his feelings of discontent and his plan to usurp Edgar's position in a soliloquy at the beginning of act 1, scene 2. He speaks of how he will act to obtain what the laws—and his father's acquiescence with these laws—deny him. Effectively disinherited through no action of his own, but by being born out of wedlock, Edmund asserts his right to succeed by claiming his brother's title and part in the kingdom: "Legitimate Edgar, I must have your land./Our father's love is to the bastard Edmund/As to the legitimate. Fine word, 'legitimate'!" (1.2.16–8).

At first glance, Edmund appears to offer a critical perspective on the kingdom and an alternative to the workings of patriarchal authority. He questions the justice of customs and laws—"the curiosity of nations"—that brand him "bastard" and "base" when his "dimensions are as well compact,/[His] mind as generous and [his] shape as true/As honest madam's issue" (1.2.7–9). He claims to see through and expose as conventional what others (most of all, Lear and Gloucester, in the earlier part of the play) call "natural"—paradigmatically, in the expression, the "offices of nature," which describes the bonds between fathers and children integral to the continuity of patrilineal succession. Against this reigning conception of what is "natural," Edmund invokes an alternative version of nature, to which he swears allegiance and for which he claims priority over "nature" exposed as convention. "Thou, Nature, art my goddess," he declares, "to thy law/My services are bound" (1.2.1–2).[25] Upon this nature beyond nature, Edmund grounds and legitimates his actions.

Edmund claims for himself, then, the status of "natural son," another name for "bastard" or "illegitimate son." Ironically, the very expression "natural son" designates the male child who is excluded from the performance of "offices of nature," who is abandoned outside of the pattern of "natural" succession. The self-contradictoriness in the usage of "natural" bespeaks the instability inherent in the effort to ground practices and conventions such as primogeniture in nature. Revealing the arbitrariness of such practices, Edmund reclaims the title of "natural son" or "bastard" from those who use the title to designate, paradoxically, the unentitled male child.

In doing so, however, instead of departing from the prevailing logic, Edmund merely repeats on his own a move that "they" who brand him bastard have already made in the patriarchal, juridical-political order. In parallel fashion, Edmund legitimates his own authority by making nature the ground of his actions, even if his is a nature beyond the nature of others, which he sees through as "custom" or "the curiosity of nations." In aligning himself with a nature beyond nature, Edmund sets himself apart from instead of *within* the political realm. Nature for Edmund—like freedom for Lear—is outside of and topologically opposed to the political realm. From the perspective of nature as Archimedean point, the political realm can appear to Edmund, then, as a whole available to mastery and manipulation. Edmund sets into motion a plot to master his lack of mastery by mimicking the very master narrative whereby the juridical-political order constitutes its integrity and purity by casting bastards outside of its framework.

What *this* bastard, who is without title or part in the political realm, wants above all is to have a title or part in the political realm. The political realm must appear to him as a stabilized hierarchy of titles and parts so that he can effectively conspire to appropriate the specific title and part he wants—that of heir to Gloucester, one step or rung away from assuming the title of Gloucester himself. Edgar and Gloucester, brother and father, appear to Edmund, then, effectively as nothing more than the bearers of the titles he wants—in theatrical terms, they are reduced to nothing more than types or characters in the political realm. In this way, Edmund denies them their humanity, as they have denied him his.[26]

As I turn now to Gloucester, I raise again a question often addressed by interpreters of the play: what makes Gloucester so easily duped by Edmund? To my above suggestion that Gloucester's gullibility has to do with his recent return from Lear's court, I add the corollary hypothesis that Gloucester is duped because he simply cannot tell the difference between his sons. Blind to their distinctness, he takes one son's character as interchangeable with the other's.

Right at the beginning of the play we hear Gloucester—between speculating about the impending spectacle and the King's arrival—speaking of his sons to Kent. Grudgingly and aversively, he introduces Edmund to his fellow courtier—

I have so often blushed to acknowledge him that now
I am brazed to't. . . .
Though this knave came something saucily
to the world before he was sent for, yet was his
mother fair, there was good sport at his making, and
the whoreson must be acknowledged.

(1.1.9–10, 20–3)

—dispatching him away in both the temporally immediate and less immediate senses. Edmund must disappear chronologically *before* the King appears so that Gloucester may appear *before*—that is, in the presence of—the King. Even prior to the King's arrival, Gloucester's remarks about Edmund already bespeak a preparation for how he should appear before the King. His presentation in court holds a priority that structures his relationship to his sons. It is principally as spectator of the King that Gloucester sees and, in a crucial way, does *not* see his sons.

If he speaks aversively of Edmund, he speaks of Edgar in barely more affectionate terms. In the same opening conversation with Kent, he remarks, "I have a son, sir, by order of law, some/year elder than this, who yet is no dearer in my account" (1.1.18–9). Gloucester differentiates between his sons here only in legal terms. If he favors Edgar, this favoritism derives solely from Edgar's legitimacy, his identity as given within the juridical-political framework. Gloucester displays an aversion not just to Edmund as illegitimate son but, more fundamentally, an aversion to seeing his sons as anything more or less than legitimate and illegitimate.

Gloucester returns home from Lear's court still reeling from what he has seen and heard. He enters muttering to himself, as quoted above, "Kent banished thus? and France in choler parted?/And the King gone tonight? Prescribed his power,/Confined to exhibition? All this done/Upon the gad?" and stops only when he sees Edmund and asks, "Edmund, how now, what news?" (1.2.23–6). Edmund pockets the letter he has forged to incriminate Edgar. Seeing Edmund hide the letter, Gloucester urgently asks, "Why so earnestly seek you to put up that/letter?" "What paper were you reading?" (1.2.27–8, 31):

EDMUND   Nothing, my lord.
GLOUCESTER   No? What needed then that terrible
dispatch of it into your pocket? The quality of nothing
hath not such need to hide itself. Let's see.—Come, if
it be nothing, I shall not need spectacles.

(1.2.32–6)

"Nothing" serves precisely to arouse Gloucester's suspicion. "Nothing" cannot be nothing, but must hide something that one needs spectacles to see. Determining *that* "nothing" hides, Gloucester is determined to see *what* "nothing" hides, unaware that his search for "what 'nothing' hides" tends to transform "that 'nothing' hides" into its very object.

Returning from one spectacle, Gloucester becomes unwittingly engaged as actor in another. "Nothing" is the signifier that reverberates from one scene to another. In the first scene, "nothing" acts as the wounding event of Lear's theater of sovereignty, the event that throws the kingdom out of joint or, rather, that exposes its essential disjointedness. In the aftermath of this unsettling event, Gloucester hears again "nothing" in his own home. As interpreter of "nothing," Gloucester attempts to reestablish mastery over the unmastering of his king's master plot. That "nothing" should mark trouble in his own home would confirm his theory of cosmic disarray, which the happenings at Lear's court he has just witnessed would symptomatically illustrate:

These late eclipses in the sun and moon
portend no good to us. Though the wisdom of Nature
can reason it thus and thus, yet nature finds itself
scourged by the sequent effects. Love cools, friendship
falls off, brothers divide: in cities, mutinies; in
    countries, discord; in palaces, treason; and the bond
cracked 'twixt son and father. This villain of mine
comes under the prediction—there's son against father.
The King falls from bias of nature—there's father
against child. We have seen the best of our time.
Machinations, hollowness, treachery and all ruinous
disorders follow us disquietly to our graves.

(1.2.103–14)

According to the perspective of this astrological explanation, which may be read as meta-theatrical commentary on act 1, scene 1, the recent happenings in the human realm would constitute irregularities that correspond to anomalies in the celestial realm. To this pattern Gloucester would expect irregularity in his own household to conform—that is, he would expect the outbreak of an irregularity that would confirm the very possibility of pattern and regularity. For one of his sons to go against the order of "natural" succession, then, would restore the very framework of intelligibility and predictability that deems such transgressions "unnatural."

One of his sons is indeed transgressing the "natural" order—the one who, excluded by the "natural" order, claims to see through its arbitrariness, mocking those who "make guilty of our disasters the sun,/the moon and the stars" (1.2.120–1). Gloucester, however, cannot tell his sons apart from each other. After reading the letter Edmund has forged, which exhorts sons to rise against the "idle and fond bondage in the/oppression of aged tyranny" (1.2.49–50), Gloucester asks, "You know the character to be your brother's?" (1.2.62). Shakespeare puns here obviously on "character" as handwriting and as disposition. Gloucester cannot tell the difference between his sons' handwriting nor their specific dispositions. Further, he cannot tell the difference between "character" as type and "character" as the disclosure of one's singular, unmistakable disposition. Seeing Edgar and Edmund as types—as, respectively, legitimate son and bastard—Gloucester is blind to the specificity that would render each unmistakable and uninterchangeable. A remark he makes later to Lear in an entirely different context, after he has literally lost his sight, poignantly alludes to and plays on the figurative blindness that motivates this misreading—"Were all thy letters suns, I could not see one" (4.6.136). His eyes turned toward the court as a mirror of heaven, Gloucester failed to see his sons.

In Edmund's forged letter, addressee and addressor switch places. Edmund writes a letter pretending to be Edgar writing to Edmund, all the while expressing in its contents thoughts he reveals as his own to the audience and reader in soliloquies and asides. With the instrument of the letter, Edmund manages effectively to trade places with Edgar. The bastard usurps the place of the legitimate, while the legitimate suffers the fate of being banished from the kingdom altogether. One finds himself with the title and part he wants in the kingdom, the other finds himself without title and part in the kingdom altogether. Toward the end of the chapter I consider the changes Edgar undergoes as a consequence and how he emerges as preeminent spectator and choric figure in the second half of the play.[27]

The Men That Follow the King

After giving up the throne Lear moves with a retinue of one hundred knights to the house of Goneril, where he thinks he will "retain/The name, and all th'addition to a king" (1.1.136–7). He is, of course, mistaken in this assumption and, soon enough, finds his orders defied and his power circumscribed. Beyond his own chain of command, he stumbles on others—precisely those he himself had created in the division of the kingdom.

Goneril and Regan order their servants not to obey him, try to regulate the behavior of his retinue, and finally divest him of his knights altogether, reducing the effects of his majesty. Lear finds that the divided kingdom is not in fact the kingdom he had planned to serve his end of freedom: the political realm does not function as a totality of titles and parts that corresponds to his will. Its members do not play the parts he had expected them to play when he asked his daughters to speak their love in exchange for property and power.

Having played the part of heir, each poises herself now to compete for the title and part of sovereign—first with Lear, and eventually against each other, moving the state step-by-step closer to civil war. Their servants, in turn, play the part of servants not to Lear but to their own mistresses. To Lear's amazement, Oswald answers his question, "who am I, sir?" not with "the King" but "[m]y lady's father" (1.4.76–7). To Lear's outrage, Cornwall dares to put Lear's servant Caius (the disguised Kent) in stocks.[28] In lieu of one central hierarchy, several centers and hierarchies vie for the supreme title and part Lear had given away.

As mentioned above, at the end of act 1, scene 1, both the play and the protagonist depart from the closed realm of ritual into the uncertain world of theater. What the play stages, however, the protagonist is slow to catch up with. From act 1, scene 3 to the end of act 2, the play shows how, in the courts of Goneril and Regan, Lear is still trapped in the realm of ritual in his peculiar position of being a king without a kingdom, while his men are in the peculiar position of following a king without a kingdom. In relation to the kingdom, Lear and his men are superfluous men. Oswald and Goneril complain that they are idle, they do not work, they perform no useful functions. All day long they eat, drink, and play.

In the divided kingdom, then, Lear and his men have become, in more than one sense, players. Their activities take place in the condition of leisure. Excessive to the realm, they have no actual titles and parts. They are itinerant and have no proper place, traveling from court to court like actors who play the part of king and king's men for those who have titles and parts and place in a court. In Goneril's household, Lear and his men constitute a kind of shadow court that both lacks and mocks the authority of her court. Unbeknownst to himself, Lear has turned into a player king and has turned his men into player men, and he is amazed to find, in the defiance of Goneril's servants and of Goneril herself, that there is now discontinuity "betwixt his sentences and his power."

Among Lear's retinue, two men—Kent and the Fool—stand out as distinct, while the hundred knights form an undifferentiated corps. Significantly, the play shows these two men explicitly and precisely as actors qua the king's men. Banished Kent returns to Lear's side with his likeness razed to play the part of Caius. And the Fool, of course, is already by definition an actor in Lear's court and continues in the divided kingdom to play the literal part of actor. What roles do they perform in relation to the king become player king, to the Lear they serve and love?

In a brief monologue at the beginning of act 1, scene 4, a disguised Kent reveals to the audience his intention to serve where he stands condemned. He returns to assume the same position in relation to Lear that he had played before Lear banished him: that of loyal servant to the master whom he loves. In the structure of his loyalty he differs from his fellow peer Gloucester, whose allegiance is oriented toward whoever occupies the formal position of master, and who is not slow to call Cornwall "[the] noble Duke, my master/My worthy arch and patron" (2.1.58–9). Kent's loyalty is ever and only to Lear, rather than dictated by a formal logic, according to which one master may be substituted for another.

While Gloucester remains silent in the first scene, Kent speaks out against Lear's repudiation of Cordelia. He begins his objection by addressing first respectfully "[r]oyal Lear,/Whom I have ever honoured as my king,/Loved as my father, as my master followed," but breaches court decorum and steps out of the master-servant relationship completely when he says, "be Kent unmannerly/When Lear is mad. What wouldst thou do, old man?" (1.1.140–3, 146–7). Poet and Shakespeare scholar John Berryman comments on this turn: "It is certain that the King can never before have been addressed as 'old man.' What this really means is that he is not King anymore. Kent . . . has sensed the vanishing of the actuality with the power; he is indifferent to the *name* of King. . . . Kent's loyalty . . . is to the *person*, whom he knows will suffer."[29] Kent follows Lear in his dispossession and displacement, taking, as the Fool puts it, "one's part that's out of favour." Banished Kent joins Lear in the latter's effective banishment of himself from the kingdom to a superfluousness he mistakes—madly—for freedom.

Kent remains loyal to Lear after opposing him; indeed, Kent remains loyal to Lear *by* opposing him. The Fool, too, remains loyal to Lear through opposition, but the structure and effect of his fidelity, as of his opposition, differ from Kent's. While Kent opposes Lear by speaking plainly and is consistently linked in the play with the motif of plain speech (he tells Cornwall in 2.2.90 "'tis my occupation to be plain"), the Fool takes another tack and opposes Lear through oblique, nonsensical speech. Through jokes, puns, riddles, and rhymes, the Fool opposes and remains loyal to Lear by estranging the King from his customary relationship to speech.

The Fool, as the following exchange implies, aims not only to delight but also to instruct:

FOOL   Sirrah, I'll teach thee a speech.
LEAR   Do.
FOOL   Mark it, nuncle:
>   Have more than thou showest,
>   Speak less than thou knowest,
>   Lend less than thou owest,
>   Ride more than thou goest,
>   Learn more than thou trowest,
>   Set less than thou throwest,
>   Leave thy drink and thy whore
>   And keep in-a-door,
>   And thou shalt have more
>   Than two cents to a score.
KENT   This is nothing, fool.
FOOL   Then 'tis like the breath of an unfee'd lawyer, you
    gave me nothing for't. [*to Lear*] Can you make no use of nothing,
    nuncle?
LEAR   Why no, boy; nothing can be made of nothing.

                                          (1.4.113–30)

What does the Fool's speech teach Lear? Or, rather, how might it constitute a teaching of the King? The Fool offers the King a ditty—a collection of proverbs about the wisdom of limits. He recites to the King a folk lesson on housekeeping whose relevance to Lear's situation is not self-evident but calls instead for interpretation. The Fool's speech constitutes, then, an invitation to the King for interpretation—a departure for a man unaccustomed to speaking and being spoken to with ambiguity, whose customary mode of speech is the imperative, which he uses to command or, failing that, to curse. To Kent's dismissive comment that "this is nothing," the Fool responds by riffing on the word itself and eliciting, through his wordplay, a repetition of the primal scene of "nothing" in the play. The Fool then restages for Lear in miniature that scene, involving him as a director would an actor:

> That lord that counselled thee to give away thy land,
> Come place him here by me; do thou for him stand.

The sweet and bitter fool will presently appear,
The one in motley here, the other found out there.
LEAR   Dost thou call me fool, boy?
FOOL   All thy other titles thou hast given away; that thou
wast born with.

(1.4.137–43)

Through this restaging, the Fool makes Lear spectator and auditor of the very scene he had staged earlier, creates for Lear the occasion of overhearing himself—and thus opens up the possibility of a difference in hearing as well as, in the legal sense, a different "hearing." "Nothing can be made of nothing" echoes Lear's reply to Cordelia: "How, nothing will come of nothing. Speak again" (1.1.90), which is itself already an echo of Cordelia's first "nothing," thus part of a series of echoes that I reproduce again below:

CORDELIA   Nothing, my lord.
LEAR   Nothing?
CORDELIA   Nothing.

(1.1.87–90)

Lear's echoing reply to Cordelia takes the form of the single word itself as a question and registers in this form his initial incomprehension. His second echo takes the form of a sentence that, having overcome incomprehension, decides already the significance of the word—an echo that, by comprehending the signifier in the sentence unit, simultaneously assimilates the signifier into a framework of comprehension. According to this framework, "nothing" has no place, is improper to, the economy of the kingdom, and for the "nothing" she speaks Cordelia will get "nothing"—that is, no part of the kingdom comprehended as a whole divisible into three or two parts without remainder. "Nothing will come of nothing" negates the alterity and *force* of Cordelia's "nothing" as an event that interrupts and opens up the logic of the kingdom as a divisible whole with the corresponding articulation of its members as subjects with titles and parts. "Nothing will come of nothing" negates Cordelia's address of love, which acts precisely in terms of a singularity in excess of title and part.

In this initial exchange between Lear and Cordelia, there emerges two ways of saying "nothing." At stake are two conceptions of freedom, as I discussed above: freedom as an end outside the political realm, and freedom as an action that takes place between human actors within the political realm and that interrupts the knowability of this realm and the articulation of identities within it. The determination of "nothing" as improper to the political realm preserves both freedom and the political realm as sovereign and intact; but, paradoxically, this sovereignty and intactness depends constitutively on the exclusion of "nothing" as haunting excess. Hence the repeated gesture of banishment throughout the play as instrument whereby sovereignty constitutes itself. Cordelia's "nothing," on the contrary, exposes the very *impropriety* of the political realm and the scandalous impropriety of the human being who, while participating in the political realm as a member with a title and part, also *exceeds* the logic of titles and parts.

Characters repeat and return to these two ways of saying "nothing" in the signifier's reverberation throughout the play. Gloucester's "quality of nothing/hath not such need to hide itself" reproduces Lear's gesture of stabilizing the force of "nothing" within a framework of comprehension, an order in which the place of self and other in relation to the kingdom is already known. The Fool's repetition of "nothing," on the other hand, bears witness to and continues through reenactment the process initiated by Cordelia of exceeding that framework of comprehension.

Nowhere mentioned in the first scene, the Fool, as commentators have long observed, enjoys special affinity with Cordelia. He is introduced as having "much pined away" since Cordelia's "going into France" (1.4.71–2), and is famously confused with Cordelia when, at the end, Lear laments, "And my poor fool is hanged" (5.3.304). The two characters are never mentioned as appearing on stage at the same time, but they perform similar functions in relation to Lear and to the kingdom. Tellingly, just as Kent intervened in Cordelia's defense in the first scene, he assumes again a similar intercessory role by commenting for Lear on the Fool's repetition of Cordelia's "nothing": "This is not altogether fool, my lord" (1.4.144).

To return to the question I posed above, what roles do Kent and the Fool perform in relation to the king become player king, to the Lear they serve and love? One has literally become an actor and the other continues to be an actor in the divided kingdom, actors in the non-court of the king who does not see what they see—namely, that he has become player king but madly expects still to be recognized as king by the members of the divided kingdom. Kent sees the reality of Lear's lack of authority and acts therefore to see *for* him and aims to help Lear restore the reality of his authority. The Fool, more radically, sees not just the reality of Lear's lack of authority but that Lear's sense of his own authority is fundamentally out of touch with reality. The Fool does not act so much to see *for* Lear as to help Lear see differently. He addresses his non-sense to Lear's sense—in an effort to bring the king to his senses beyond the madness of his sense.

In remaining loyal to and following Lear, Kent and the Fool both maintain relationships to Cordelia. Kent's loyalty to Lear entails keeping Lear open to Cordelia and guarding this openness; Kent will indeed act as the mediating agent who brings Cordelia back from France to aid Lear. The Fool's loyalty to Lear is also inflected by a fundamental fidelity to Cordelia. He acts Cordelia's part in relation to Lear—the part of having no part or title in the kingdom, of continuing the process she initiated with her event of "nothing," an event that, interrupting the rules and structure of Lear's theater of sovereignty, opened up a radical new possibility within the kingdom.

On the Heath: The Tragedy of (Non-)Exposure

At the end of act 2, Lear leaves the house of Regan and Cornwall with a retinue that has dwindled to only Kent and the Fool as a storm builds over the heath. This departure effectively realizes the condition of superfluousness to which Lear had relegated himself and his men without knowing it, a superfluousness in which freedom is indistinguishable from banishment in being likewise situated outside the political realm. The very effort to stabilize the kingdom and its members in accordance with a sovereign perspective results in abandonment on the very site that serves, as exceptional site within the kingdom, to guarantee the topology of sovereignty and constitute the kingdom's integrity. Midway into its unfolding, in the first half of act 3, the play moves to this site. The stage becomes a heath on which characters find themselves outside of political space and exposed to the elements. In showing the characters' exposure to the elements, however, the play shows that the characters thereby avoid precisely *being exposed to each other,* and thus remain tragically caught within a sovereign determination of the human. While showing us the failure of the characters to be exposed to each other, I argue, the play begins to expose us, its readers and spectators, with proto-Artaudian cruelty to the possibility of a new, non-sovereign logic of spectatorship. Like Cordelia and the Fool, the play interrupts in its second half the rules and structure of the theater of sovereignty to open up within the ruins of this theater the possibility of a non-sovereign politics and aesthetics.

The heath thus serves as a site of transformation—not so much of the relationships between the characters within the play as of the relationship of the play to the audience. Serving such a function, the heath may be compared to what critics call, after Northrop Frye, the "green world" in Shakespearean comedy, a space of exile and errancy in which the normal political order is suspended, identities of characters exchanged and transformed, and the kingdom thereby regenerated.[30] Taking after the archetype of the wasteland, the heath is anti-type to the fertile, life-affirming green world: it does not serve as site of regeneration for the characters or of the kingdom. Nevertheless, the heath serves as watershed to the extent that the play begins thereafter itself to transform.

An obvious way in which the heath serves as watershed is that, for the first time, the subplot significantly converges with the Lear plot after more or less running parallel up to this point. On the heath, Lear encounters Edgar disguised as "Poor Tom," the proverbial name given to a wandering Bedlam beggar. On the heath Gloucester decides to offer shelter to Lear, the Fool, and Kent after first wavering in his allegiance. In the meantime, Edmund begins to conspire with Goneril, Cornwall, and Regan in the hope of taking their fathers' respective titles and parts in the kingdom, a process that leads to Gloucester's blinding at the end of act 3.

I examine now the first of these convergences: Lear's encounter with Edgar as "Poor Tom." On the heath, the unhoused Lear is exposed to the elements, raging, like Job, "a man / More sinn'd against than sinning" (3.2.58–9), with no one to respond to his cries but the storm. He is persuaded by Kent to seek shelter in a hovel, where they encounter an unclothed madman who speaks incessantly of the cold and who addresses, instead of human interlocutors, fiends. Unbeknownst to Lear and Kent, this is Edgar. Significantly, as a consequence of this encounter Lear goes mad and will not regain his senses until the end of act 4, when he wakes to recognize Cordelia.

Right before entering the hovel on the heath, Lear imagines and addresses a stratum of subjects in his kingdom so low they had hitherto escaped his notice:

> Poor naked wretches, where so'er you are,
> That bide the pelting of this pitiless storm,
> How shall your houseless heads and unfed sides,
> Your loop'd and window'd raggedness, defend you
> From seasons such as these? O! I have ta'en
> Too little care of this. Take physic, Pomp;
> Expose thyself to feel what wretches feel,
> That thou mayst shake the superflux to them,
> And show the Heavens more just.

$$(3.4.28–36)$$

As if in answer to his invocation, Poor Tom immediately makes his appearance, covered by nothing more than a blanket. Lear's first words to this apparition are: "Didst thou give all to thy daughters?/And art thou come to this?" (3.4.48–9). Even after Kent tries to correct him by telling him, "He hath no daughters, Sir," Lear insists with righteous indignation, "Death, traitor! nothing could have subdu'd nature/To such a lowness but his unkind daughters" (3.4.69–70). Lear projects onto Poor Tom an image of his own diminished state and would impress on his followers the same vision. The sight induces in him the following famous disquisition:

> Thou wert better in a grave than to answer
> with thy uncovered body this extremity of the skies
> Is man no more than this? Consider him well. Thou
> ow'st the worm no silk, the beast no hide, the sheep
> no wool, the cat no perfume. Ha? Here's three on's
> us are sophisticated; thou art the thing itself.
> Unaccommodated man is no more but such a poor,
> bare, forked animal as thou art. Off, off, you lendings:
> come, unbutton here.
>
> (3.4.99–107)

At the end of this speech, Lear tears off his clothes: he begins to resemble Poor Tom physically as well as mentally, identifying with what he sees as a specimen of naked life outside of political life.

What does Lear see in Poor Tom? He claims to see the "thing itself," "unaccommodated man," "a poor, bare, forked animal." Tom appears to him as an exhibit of human life exposed to the elements, unqualified by participation in the political realm, barely distinguishable from animal life. In attempting to tear off his clothes, Lear seems to think that he discovers his own nakedness symmetrically in the nakedness of Poor Tom. Lear seems to think, then, that he has discovered who or *what* he is—bare, unaccommodated man—and thus resolved the crisis of identity he has been suffering since his abdication. "Who am I, sir?" he asks Oswald in act 1. Oswald's reply, "My lady's father," triggers incredulity and invective from Lear: "My lady's father? My lord's knave, you whoreson/dog, you slave, you cur!" (1.4.76–9). Lear seems to think that he now has the answer to the question "Who am I, sir?" in the image of Poor Tom that is produced a little too conveniently, as if by royal fiat, in quick response to his command, "Take physic, Pomp;/Expose thyself to feel what wretches feel." Poor Tom appears as a pageant-like display that reflects the sovereign gaze, a tableau of "unaccommodated man" that Lear directs Kent and the Fool to see in the same way with the imperative, "Consider him well."

In Poor Tom Lear thinks he has discovered the image of what it is to be a man without title or part in the kingdom—that is, the outcast as bare unaccommodated man. At the same time, in Poor Tom Edgar too thinks he has discovered the part of what it is to be without title or part, for Poor Tom is literally the part Edgar chooses to play of having no title or part in the kingdom, the part of the outcast in the theater of sovereignty that is being curiously staged between himself and Lear on the heath.

Edgar appears at first in the play as a simple character who accepts without question his part in the kingdom as heir to Gloucester's title—and the corresponding articulation of others, including the exclusion of his bastard brother, in relation to his position as given within the "natural order." This simpleton accepts unproblematically what Edmund tells him, and thus falls victim to his envious brother's machinations and his gullible father's complacency. It is only in banishment that Edgar begins to show independence in his thinking, becoming the character who more than all others speaks in soliloquies and asides, revealing a separate interiority and emerging as preeminent mediating perspective for reader and audience. In banishment Edgar also becomes literally an actor, assuming a series of disguises that represents a gradual but unmistakable ascension of the sociopolitical hierarchy that ends with his reclaiming the title of Gloucester after his duel with Edmund.

Banished by his father from the kingdom, hunted by men who would kill him, Edgar decides, like Kent, to remain within the kingdom by adopting disguise. But if Kent is motivated primarily by his personal loyalty to Lear to take the part of Caius, the same part he had played in relation to Lear before his banishment, Edgar is motivated to adopt disguise primarily by a desire for the restitution of his name, a restitution that involves, necessarily, revenge. "I am no less in blood than thou art, Edmund; / If more, the more thou'st wronged me. / My name is Edgar and thy father's son" (5.3.165–7), he tells his brother after defeating him in their final duel. Edgar's attachment to his name entails attachment to the formal, juridical-political structure, the "natural" or legitimate order, in which the name of Edgar coincides with entitlement to the title of Gloucester.

Banishment situates Edgar outside of that "natural order" altogether. Edgar loses his title to the usurping Edmund and effectively, in multiple senses, changes places with Edmund, with the two brothers becoming doubles of each other. For what is restitution but a symmetrical reversal of usurpation? In his opening soliloquy, Edmund grounds and legitimates his plot of usurpation in a nature beyond the "natural order" that he sees through as merely arbitrary and conventional. This affirmation of a nature beyond nature gives him an Archimedean point whereby the political realm can appear to him as a whole available to mastery and manipulation. For Edmund, Edgar and Gloucester appear effectively as nothing more than the bearers of the titles he wants—in theatrical terms, nothing more than types or characters in the political realm. Edmund's plot of usurpation thus mimics and participates in the very logic whereby the juridical-political order constitutes itself as sovereign whole by banishing bastards outside its framework.

Banished, Edgar finds himself in relation to the kingdom in the position Edmund had occupied before. He too views the kingdom as a totality of titles and parts from which he is excluded, although his perspective on the kingdom affords a pronouncedly more vertical view than Edmund's. His plot of restitution entails playing a series of ascending parts in the kingdom—Poor Tom, a peasant when he leads Gloucester, the verbal disguise of a West Country yokel when he kills Oswald, the masked stranger who challenges Edmund to a duel—on his way back to reclaiming his "rightful" title and part. He begins the process by playing what he considers the "basest" part. In his first soliloquy in the play, he explains his strategy:

> I heard myself proclaimed,
> And by the happy hollow of a tree
> Escaped the hunt. No port is free, no place
> That guard and most unusual vigilance
> Does not attend my taking. While I may scape
> I will preserve myself, and am bethought
> To take the basest and most poorest shape
> That ever penury in contempt of man
> Brought near to beast. My face I'll grime with filth,
> Blanket my loins, elf all my hair in knots
> And with presented nakedness outface
> The winds and persecutions of the sky.
> The country gives me proof and precedent
> Of Bedlam beggars, who, with roaring voices,
> Strike in their numbed and mortified bare arms
> Pins, wooden pricks, nails, sprigs of rosemary;
> And with this horrible object, from low farms,
> Poor pelting villages, sheepcotes and mills,
> Sometime with lunatic bans, sometime with prayers,

Enforce their charity. Poor Turlygod, poor Tom,
That's something yet: Edgar I nothing am.

(2.2.172–92)

This speech is framed by two remarks that indicate Edgar's estrangement from himself—that is, from himself qua the title and part once marked by the name "Edgar" but now occupied by the name "Edmund" in the disintegrating political order. In the remark "I heard myself proclaimed," Edgar becomes a new grammatical subject capable of beholding from a distance his former status as if the latter were an object. Banished Edgar now views the kingdom theatrically—as a constellation of parts, in which his part has now been taken by another actor. The legalistic language of "proof and precedent" he uses to justify his choice of a new part suggests the degree to which his theatrical view of the kingdom coincides with its juridical-political articulation. "Edgar I nothing am," he states; his role has been taken, and he is nothing apart from that role. Edgar subscribes to the notion that to be something or someone is necessarily to have a title or role, even if it entails playing the part of having no title or part—the part of Poor Tom.

To play the part of Poor Tom is to substantialize the condition of banishment as an identity, to assume an identity recognizable to the sovereign gaze as, paradoxically, the identity of not having an identity within the kingdom. To do so, then, is to turn nothing into something, and to negate the force of "nothing" as an action or event that precisely interrupts the logic of the kingdom as a sovereign totality of titles and parts and that thus opens up the possibility of a new political logic. In playing Poor Tom, Edgar plays the part of having no title or part in the kingdom in a way that confirms and perpetuates the rules and structure of the existing situation. In contradistinction, the event of Cordelia's "nothing" and the Fool's fidelity to this event perform the part of having no title or part in the kingdom by interrupting the logic of sovereignty and exposing the human being's irreducibility to title or part, type or character; his radical noncoincidence with any given identity; his radical unknowability to others and to himself; his singularity.

In the part of Poor Tom, Edgar will "with presented nakedness outface / The winds and persecutions of the sky." It is this part of presented nakedness that Lear encounters in the hovel and takes to show what man fundamentally is: "un-/accommodated man is no more but such a poor,/bare, forked animal as thou art" (3.4.104–6). But Lear makes here a mistake, which I'll begin explaining with reference to what Stanley Cavell in *The Claim of Reason* terms, after Thoreau and Dickens, the "problem of the humanitarian":

"The problem of the humanitarian is not merely that his acts of acknowl-edgment are too thin, mere assuagings of guilt; but that they are apt, even bound, to confusion. His intention is to acknowledge the outcast as a human being; but his effect is to treat a human being as an outcast, as if the condition of outcastness defined a social role, a kind of sub-profession, suited for a certain kind of human being."[31] My gloss on Cavell's remarks is that Lear identifies with Poor Tom as outcast in an attempt to stabilize what the human being is, but his very attempt to stabilize what the human being is constitutes a denial of the human being's humanity. Edgar is in the encounter partner to this very confusion and denial.

In the encounter between Lear and Poor Tom, the play shows the audi-ence more than what Lear sees. However, readers and audiences have been curiously inclined *not* to see more than Lear sees, but to see *just as* he sees and commands others to see: namely, to consider Poor Tom as an exem-plum of the bare animal or brute body that, according to this logic of seeing, forms the substance or base—or, in arithmetical terms, denominator com-mon to king and beggar alike—which under our lendings we share with each other as human beings. Under their clothes, the king is the equal of the beggar. The king, like the beggar, is not "ague-proof" (4.6.107). And it is tempting in turn to see in Lear, when he tears off his lendings, the very image of what Lear sees in Tom, to repeat Lear's seeing of Tom in the seeing of Lear. To participate in such humanitarian seeing, and in the pity it gener-ates, is to miss or dismiss, however, that the play shows the nakedness of Poor Tom as a "*presented* nakedness," that Edgar hypostatizes the condition of the outcast in a way that arrests and screens genuine exposure to the humanity of the other, a humanity that essentially resists any attempt at stabilization.

By abdicating and dividing the kingdom before his death, Lear becomes a man without title or part in the kingdom, mistakenly thinking that he would enjoy a supra-role in relation to the kingdom that would serve his end of freedom. On the heath, in the encounter with Poor Tom, Lear thinks that he has rediscovered what it is to be a man without title or part in the kingdom, but once again he is mistaken. By abdicating before his death, Lear divides what must, according to the medieval and early modern doctrine of the king's two bodies, remain indivisible. As the Elizabethan jurist Edmund Plowden writes in his *Reports*:

> For the King has in him two Bodies, *viz.*, a Body natural and a Body politic. His Body natural . . . is a Body mortal, subject to all Infirmities that come

by Nature or Accident, to the Imbecility of Infancy or old Age, and to the like defects that happen to the natural Bodies of other People. But his Body politic is a Body that cannot be seen or handled, consisting of Policy and Government, and constituted for the Direction of the People, and the Management of the public weal, and this Body is utterly void of Infancy, and old Age, and other natural Defects and Imbecilities, which the Body natural is subject to.[32]

In the king the body politic and the body natural are incorporated in one person and indivisible. Only upon the king's death does the body natural divide from the body politic. As the familiar saying goes, "The King is dead! Long live the King!" The doctrine of the king's two bodies insists on the immortality of the body politic that survives the finitude of successive kings—an immortality that serves as the earthly version of the immortality of God, and vice versa. Lear, however, violates the indivisibility of the king's two bodies before his death. If it were a case of simple arithmetic, in which the king's two bodies constituted two halves of a whole, then what Lear would be left with after division is the body natural—the mortal body that he has in common with all other human beings, but not just all other human beings but all other living beings, including plants and animals.

To claim a common ground for human life in a shared biological finitude, then, would be to elide the distinction between human life and plant and animal life, and thus to deny the specificity of human life. As philosopher Giorgio Agamben has argued in his studies of sovereignty in Western political thought, this mistake has been made persistently, even across the transition from monarchical government to representative democracy as paradigmatic form of government in secular modernity. In the modern, liberal democratic assumption of the separability of "man" from "citizen," sovereignty continues, in the form of representative governments instead of monarchies, to constitute its legitimacy and power over the "bare life" of human beings. The concentration camp inmate and the refugee are examples, according to Agamben, of the nation-state's exclusion of "bare life" from its borders, an exclusion predicated on the separability of "man" from "citizen," on the possibility of isolating human life as extra-political animal life from human life as always already political form-of-life.[33]

Lear and Edgar, in identifying with and taking the part of excluded bare life, then, paradoxically confirm the very sovereign logic whereby they have been cast out of the kingdom. In making "Poor Tom" the "base" or foundation of an extra-political human life, they underwrite the separability of human life from political life, the possibility of its exposure outside political life. In doing so, they participate in an equation of human life with biological finitude that denies the human being's specific humanity.

The human being is, of course, an animal; but specifically the human being is, in Aristotle's formulation in the *Politics*, an animal or living being that has speech—*zoon logon echon*.[34] Like plants and animals, human beings are biologically alive, and sustain themselves through biological processes, and, like plants and animals, are capable of extending the species through biological reproduction. But human beings, unlike other living things, are capable of reproducing themselves not just biologically but through speech and action, and thereby to constitute a specifically human world that survives the finitude of individuals and successive generations. Every human being, according to Hannah Arendt in *The Human Condition*, necessarily undergoes beyond biological birth a second birth into the human world as a complex animal that has speech, and is capable of speech and action. She enters the human world of speech and action that precedes her and that will survive her; and, while she may inherit in the world that precedes her a given part, she is capable of acting beyond that part and inaugurating a new process in the world that has, by definition, unpredictable consequences.[35]

How does the living being become the living being that has speech? How does this transition take place, and what is its structure? The Greeks have two words for "life": *zoe*, which expresses the simple fact of living common to all living beings; and *bios*, which designates the way of life proper to an individual or a group. Animals live, but only the human animal can, by living together with others in the polis—that is, as a political animal—live well and deliberate with others the affairs they have in common. As an animal that deliberates with others and gives reasons, the human being has language and not merely voice (*phone*), which other animals likewise use to express pleasure and pain. Agamben writes in *Homo Sacer*: "The question 'In what way does the living being have language?' corresponds exactly to the question 'In what way does bare life dwell in the *polis*?' The living being has *logos* by taking away and conserving its own voice [*phone*] in it, even as it dwells in the *polis* by letting its own bare life be excluded, as an exception, within it."[36] On Agamben's analogy between the articulation *phone-logos* and *zoe-bios*, the Slovenian philosopher and cultural critic Mladen Dolar comments:

> Voice is like bare life, something that is supposedly exterior to the political, while *logos* is the counterpart of *polis*, of social life ruled by laws and the

common good. But the whole point . . . is, of course, that there is no such simple externality: the basic structure, the topology of the political, is for Agamben that of an "inclusive exclusion" of naked life. This very exclusion places *zoe* in a central and paradoxical place; the exception falls into interiority. . . . For what presents a problem is not that *zoe* is simply presocial, the animality, the outside of the social, but that it persists, in its very exclusion/inclusion, at the heart of the social—just as the voice is not simply an element external to speech, but persists at its core, making it possible and constantly haunting it by the impossibility of symbolizing it.[37]

While bare life is excluded for the very constitution of political life, it is not simply outside the polis but uncannily internal to the polis as an inclusive exclusion, just as voice is not pre- or extra-linguistic but uncannily that through whose inclusive exclusion language is at all possible. Sovereign thinking has traditionally regarded bare life as simply external to the polis, and voice as simply external to language. This mistake converts complexity into binary opposition, severing the complex knot whereby bare life constitutively inhabits the polis and voice uncannily haunts language. Through the institution of a simple inside/outside topology, sovereignty can establish and affirm its own integrity and dominion vis-à-vis bare life and set parameters around speech by eliminating as nonsense the excess of voice within speech.

The instrument of sovereignty is banishment. Sovereignty maintains itself by casting out, exposing human life as bare life outside the political realm. In so doing, it represses and finds a substitute for a more fundamental exposure that is already part of the political realm—that is, indeed, constitutively part of the human being's being part of the political realm. Call it exposure as exposure to others in the human world as an always already political realm for which there is no outside. Exposure qua exposure to others is condition and ongoing process of the human being's second birth into the human world as a being capable of speech and action in being with and among others. Such exposure implies that one's perspective is one among many *in* the world, and cannot thus be a perspective *on* the world as a unity and *on* the many in the world as members of a finite and stable unity of parts. Such exposure implies also that one's perspective is not itself a unitary part of a unity but essentially not-one, radically incomplete and dependent on the perspectives of others that are mutually exposed to each other.

In the world among others, the human being exists in a condition of plurality prior to the emergence as abstraction of the one from this originary situation. As Arendt writes, "No man can be sovereign because not one man, but men, inhabit the earth."[38] In being among others, no one can have perspective on the whole, nor can plurality amount to a whole, since the "whole"—call it the world—is that which is interminably and infinitely created through the exposure of human beings to each other—and thus is precisely not-whole.

In taking the part of the outcast, Lear and Edgar endorse the sovereign logic of exposure outside the political realm as whole. The part of Poor Tom functions as a screen that shows a false image to each of who he "is"— the part that has no part or title in the kingdom—and thus blocks them from genuine exposure to each other. The play shows the recognition of what man is in Poor Tom—a bare, poor, forked creature—as, ironically, a mis-recognition. The theater of sovereignty that takes place on the heath is, in these terms, a tragedy of non-exposure.

Consequent to this encounter the king goes mad and will only regain his senses in act 4 by means of two recognitions—of Gloucester and Cordelia. Consequent to this encounter, another significant turn takes place in the play—a turn not so much on the level of plot as on the level of what is called "meta-theater." From this point on, Edgar becomes the chief choric figure, the surrogate spectator who comments in asides and soliloquies on the suffering of other characters and the interactions between them—all the while advancing in disguise his plot to reclaim his title and part in the king-dom, emerging as the hero of the subplot become revenge tragedy. Edgar acquires such prominence in the play that the 1608 Quarto titles the play the "True Chronicle Historie of the life and death of King Lear and his three Daughters. With the unfortunate life of Edgar, Sonne and heire to the Earle of Gloster, and his sullen and assumed humor of Tom of Bedlam."[39]

What is the impact for the reader or spectator of these turns—the mad-ness of the king and the surrogate spectatorship of Edgar? And what is the relationship between them? I pursue these questions in the final sections of this chapter.

The Losing and Refinding of the Sense(s)

By the end of the heath scene, Lear has gone mad, but he will recover his senses sufficiently to recognize Gloucester in act 4, scene 6 and Cordelia in scene 7. His recovery will be tentative and short-lived, however, as the events of his capture and Cordelia's death arrest again his claim on reality before the end of the play. I propose in this section to examine how, through the recognitions of Gloucester and Cordelia, Lear finds his senses again and his way back to the world as a world lived, however precariously, among others. I reconsider in my investigation Cavell's argument in "The Avoidance of Love" that the condition of Lear's recognition of others is that he allow himself first to be recognized by them, that he accept his being-among-others as radically and essentially an exposure-to-others. In the following section, I would then like to discuss the complex ways in which the play, in the very process of showing Lear's losing and refinding of his senses, elliptically involves *us*—the readers and spectators—in a dramatic losing and refinding of our senses.

In such colloquial expressions as "losing one's senses" or "coming to one's senses," the plural term "senses" is semantically almost interchangeable with the singular term "sense." This semantic proximity attests to the strength of the relationship between the five senses—vision, hearing, taste, touch, and smell—and "sense" in the singular, a relationship that the philosophical tradition has articulated in terms of the division between the sensible and the intelligible. Sense in the singular has, in the Platonic-Cartesian tradition, been accorded a privileged position in relation to the plural senses, which have been construed as the portals through which the mind receives data that it processes to "make sense." The mind demonstrates its separateness from and transcendence of the phenomenal world in its capacity for such abstract operations as mathematical thought or remembrance, reflection, and imagination—in short, in its capacity to *think* in isolation from the world of appearances.

For the Platonic-Cartesian tradition, the capacity of the mind to think in isolation from the phenomenal world gives evidence of what is immortal in men, connecting finite individuals to a dimension that transcends them as well as the mere sensible world in which they appear to each other. From the perspective of the thinking ego, the world of appearances is a world of mere semblance or illusion, whose existence cannot even be affirmed with certainty. Truth is, in this schema, situated outside the world of appearances and is, as such, opposed to mere "common sense," a form of thinking that both guides and derives from our everyday, practical life in the world of appearances. Regarded with suspicion from the perspective of truth, common sense does not maintain the strict hierarchical division between the sensible and the intelligible.

The abstraction of the thinking subject from the world of appearances rests on a denial of the priority for human beings of the world as au fond a world of appearances. Hannah Arendt writes in her introductory remarks on the world's phenomenal nature in *The Life of the Mind*:

> The world men are born into contains many things, natural and artificial, living and dead, transient and sempiternal, all of which have in common that they *appear* and hence are meant to be seen, heard, touched, tasted, and smelled, to be perceived by sentient creatures endowed with the appropriate sense organs. In this world which we enter, appearing from a nowhere, and from which we disappear into a nowhere, *Being and Appearing coincide.* . . . Nothing and nobody exists in this world whose very being does not presuppose a *spectator.* In other words, nothing that is, insofar as it appears, exists in the singular; everything that is is meant to be perceived by somebody. Not Man but men inhabit this planet. Plurality is the law of the earth.[40]

In Arendt's challenge to the metaphysical tradition, the human condition is fundamentally plural. Because human life is essentially plural, the very thinking of what thinking is must necessarily start from the situation of the human being as appearing in a world that likewise appears to her—from the point of view of what philosophy has traditionally designated the realm of the sensible.

What kind of point of view is a point of view situated within the realm of the sensible? According to what kind of logic does such appearing take place? Implicit in my formulation of the first question is already the long-standing privileging of vision in the Platonic-Cartesian tradition as central among the five senses. Plato's *eide* are figured as objects of visual apprehension, and in the Cartesian model the intellect "inspects" representations that are in the mind. Our vocabulary for thinking is permeated by visual metaphors: "reflection," "speculation," "observation," "insight," "imagination," "point of view," and so forth. The privileging of vision over the other senses works in tandem with the classical elevation of the intelligible over the sensible.

The second half of *King Lear*, I contend, dramatizes precisely the question: what kind of point of view is a point of view that is situated within the world as essentially a world of appearances? I'd like to suggest briefly before returning to the play that this point of view involves a reorganization of the relationship between the senses that displaces the governing centrality of vision. In more than one "sense," then, Lear must lose his senses before he can find them again to reappear in a world that does not appear to him simply according to the logic of the sovereign perspective.

The trajectory of Lear's slide into madness is attended all along by a corollary crisis of vision, which informs the so-called sight pattern that encompasses, besides Lear, almost all the other characters of the play. In banishing Cordelia and Kent, Lear clears them out of his field of vision: "Hence and avoid my sight," he orders Cordelia (1.1.125). To Kent he cries, "Out of my sight!"—to which Kent replies, "See better, Lear, and let me still remain/The true blank of thine eye" (1.1.158–60). Lear and Gloucester, the fathers in the play, will not brook obstacles to their lines of sight, but must establish their authority as all-seeing. "Let's see," Gloucester asks Edmund for his forged letter, "if it be nothing, I shall not need spectacles" (1.2.35–6). Paternal authority needs to make nothing into something it can rule over and, if necessary, banish from its field of vision.

Lear first introduces the play's motif of plucking out eyes when he finds himself—to his surprise—most *uncharacteristically*—weeping. After Goneril has reduced his retinue from one hundred to fifty, Lear tells her:

> Life and death, I am ashamed
> That thou hast power to shake my manhood thus,
> That these hot tears, which break from me perforce
> Should make thee worth them. Blasts and fogs upon thee!
> Th'untented woundings of a father's curse
> Pierce every sense about thee. Old fond eyes,
> Beweep this cause again, I'll pluck ye out,
> And cast you with the waters that you loose
> To temper clay.
>
> (1.4.288–96)

This speech marks a transition in the play. On the level of plot, Lear decides he will move from Goneril's court to Regan's, mistakenly thinking that this other daughter "is kind and comfortable" (1.4.298). On the level of Lear's speech habits, he switches at this moment from commands to curses. From his perspective, the world that had heeded his beck and call has turned against him. Therefore, if he does not have the power to command the world, he will at least exercise the power to curse it. By means of this switch, he tries precisely to maintain continuity between his sentence and his power—a continuity that serves to deny that he no longer effectively occupies the title and role of king. In the divided kingdom, Lear has become player king. His tears, however, belie his effort, via the "father's curse," to remain *in character* and to maintain his power against the claim to power of Goneril. His tears are the sign of the strain of this effort; they are the sign of his shame. His tears of shame expose the division between *who* he is and the character he wants to play, a man without title and part who enjoys a supra-role of sovereign freedom in relation to the kingdom. His tears expose *who* he is, indeed, *as* this very dividedness, a man who, being *among others* in the kingdom, can never be *one* or *at one with* having a title and part.[41] These tears also occasion precisely the process of Lear's losing of his senses.

The outbreak of tears compromises the integrity of the body's boundaries and the primacy of vision among the senses. In the expression, "[t]h'un-tented woundings of a father's curse / Pierce every sense about thee," Lear wishes for Goneril what he finds happening to himself as he cries. He would rather not have eyes at all than have eyes that, in weeping, constitute an obstacle to their capacity to see. The very attempt to deny the eyes' capacity to weep in an attempt to assert the integrity of their seeing is symptom and cause of his madness. Leaving Goneril's house, Lear mutters, "O let me not be mad, not mad, sweet heaven! I / would not be mad. / Keep me in temper, I would not be mad" (1.5.43–5). Leaving Regan's house, he cries to the assembled audience of his two daughters, Cornwall, their servants, and what remains of his retinue: "You think I'll weep, / No, I'll not weep. / I have full cause of weeping, but this heart / Shall break into a hundred thou-sand flaws / Or e'er I'll weep. O fool, I shall go mad" (2.2.471–5). The very attempt to assert his sovereignty over his eyes, and by implication his eyes' sovereignty over the other senses, is precisely what leads him to lose his senses.

Lear's recovery of his senses takes place via the recognition of Gloucester, the character who suffers in Lear's place the fate of having his eyes plucked out. Regan and Cornwall carry out the act of putting out Gloucester's eyes, but it is Goneril who suggests the punishment. Upon finding that Glouces-ter is providing a channel for Lear to the French forces landing at Dover, Regan cries, "Hang him instantly!" while Goneril offers, "Pluck out his eyes!" (3.7.4–5). Where has Goneril—and where have we—heard this expression before but from Lear, when he tells her he would rather pluck out his eyes than have them weep on her account again? Goneril echoes Lear, then, when she makes this proposal. Gloucester next unwittingly joins the chain of echoes in a way that connects his own eyes to Lear's. "I would not see thy cruel nails," he tells Cornwall and Regan, "[p]luck out his poor old eyes; nor thy fierce sister / In his anointed flesh stick boarish fangs. / . . . / but I shall see / The winged vengeance overtake such children" (3.7.55–7, 64–5). "See't shalt thou never," Cornwall rejoins and proceeds to make good on his word (3.7.66).

According to this last exchange, Gloucester is blinded so that he will not be able to see the harm planned for Lear or the fate he himself wishes upon the perpetrators. He is blinded so that he cannot be an eyewitness to Lear's undoing at the hands of those who compete to replace him as bearer of the title and part he had given away. From the perspective of the perpetrators who pretend to the title of king, Gloucester is guilty of treason, allied with Lear not as king but as enemy king and with France turned enemy state. Gloucester is punished, then, for his status as subject of Lear—punished with blinding for his insistence on the use of his eyes to see *for Lear* the restoration of the "natural" or legitimate order that Lear himself had set off course. Simultaneously, Gloucester's blinding serves the perpetrators as prelude to the death of the king that has not yet taken place but must take place so that he can be replaced—so that, in keeping with the logic of sovereign succession, the kingdom can hail, "The King is dead! Long live the King!"—so that the perpetrators can legitimate the sovereign power that, paradoxically, they already pretend to have in declaring Gloucester "traitor" and blinding him.

Gloucester's hollow eyes are sign of the collapse of the sovereign order under Lear and of the competing claims to sovereignty in the divided kingdom that has now devolved into a state of civil war. Gloucester's eyes serve as site and spoils of civil war itself, with pretenders to the title of king legitimating themselves by criminalizing the witness of the old regime, targeting the very organs most associated with witnessing, and banishing the sightless man out of their sight as he himself had earlier banished Edgar and as Lear had earlier banished Cordelia and Kent. Cornwall and Regan are the latest and bloodiest practitioners of the forcible determination of what it is to be member of and spectator in the kingdom.

The tragedy shows how civil war expresses itself as a struggle for sovereign recognition among divisions that each claims to represent the kingdom as a whole. Gloucester is blinded for recognizing the wrong sovereign by those who compete to be recognized as the next and rightful sovereign. In such competition, sovereignty reduplicates itself by creating parallel instead of successive hierarchies. An instance of this reduplication is the production of two Gloucesters—Cornwall names Edgar "Earl of Gloucester" in act 3, scene 5—who exist at the same time and bear the same title and part but in competing hierarchies that each seeks to occupy, but is incongruent with, the kingdom as a whole. Time itself is out of joint in civil war's theater of sovereignties. Yet, through Gloucester's blinding, an alternative mode of spectatorship—one that involves a new relationship of seeing to the other senses—takes place in the play. Beyond the theater of sovereign recognition, what kind of recognition takes place between blind Gloucester and mad Lear when they reappear to each other in act 4, scene 6?

The encounter is framed for the audience by Edgar, who has at this point just shed his Poor Tom disguise to adopt another, anonymous part as guide to his blind father. Edgar comments on what he and the audience can see, and the reader imagine, but that Gloucester cannot—the mad king wearing a crown of flowering weeds: "But who comes here?/The safer sense will ne'er accommodate/His master thus" (4.6.81–2).

As if having overheard the question, Lear replies, "No, they cannot touch me for coining. I am the King himself" (4.6.83–4). He utters a series of non sequiturs—"Nature's above art in that respect. There's your/press-money. That fellow handles his bow like a crow-/keeper. . . ."—that ends with the imperative, "Give the word" (4.6.92). Edgar replies, "Sweet marjoram"—which, as the editor R. A. Foakes observes, is the name for an herb that was believed to cure "cold diseases of the braine and head."[42] When Lear says, "Pass," Gloucester remarks, "I know that voice" (4.6.93–4).

After his preliminary exchange with Lear, Edgar will retreat to the wings and confine his role to such choric asides as "I would not take this from report: it is,/And my heart breaks at it" (4.6.137–8); and "O matter and impertinency mixed,/Reason in madness" (4.6.170–1). He withdraws to become spectator of the scene in which Lear and Gloucester figure in the foreground as actors. By the end of their encounter, when Cordelia's men come to escort Lear to her, Lear has recovered his senses sufficiently to say to Gloucester, "I know thee well enough, thy name is Gloucester" (4.6.173). What has transpired for this recovery to take place?

In his essay "Words and Wounds," Geoffrey Hartman memorably interprets Edgar's password, "sweet marjoram," as initiating Lear's process of healing.[43] Edgar's retreat to the wings, however, indicates that *his* words alone do not suffice to return Lear to his senses. Edgar's words preface or frame, rather, a recovery that Gloucester makes possible. What accounts for Gloucester's efficacy? I explore this question by distinguishing first the manner of Edgar's speaking with Lear from the way Gloucester speaks to Lear.

Significantly, while Edgar participates in Lear's speech, he does not *speak to* Lear. Edgar sees and hears Lear, and he responds to Lear's speech, but he does not address or reply to Lear himself. At the cue, "Give the word," he fills in the blank of Lear's speech by saying, "Sweet marjoram." While these signifiers may suggest a therapeutic dimension, they do so constatively as diagnosis rather than as action. Speech remains impersonal between the disguised Edgar and mad Lear, neither of whom addresses the other as subject of his speech. In this sense, these (non-)interlocutors resume the dialogue they had left off when Lear had just gone mad and Edgar was still disguised as Poor Tom. Speech is exchanged between them, but it does not *make a difference*, does not constitute an event between speakers.

Gloucester has been listening to this exchange in the meantime and, when he speaks, first remarks, "I know that voice," then—hearing more— "The trick of that voice I do well remember:/Is't not the King?" (4.6.95, 105–6). Gloucester cannot see that it is the King, nor can he tell from the content of Lear's speech that it is he, but it is Lear's voice that prompts him to hazard the question, "Is't not the King?" Being blind, Gloucester cannot recognize the King as he has been accustomed to do. Being mad, Lear does not speak and make sense like the King that Gloucester knew. Neither can *see*, in either the literal or figurative sense. In the derangement of the senses, the circuit of recognition between subject and sovereign is disrupted. This disruption begins to manifest itself—like a crack in the mirror of sovereignty—in the question Gloucester addresses to the man whose voice he thinks might be the King's.

The question is formulated in the third person. It addresses Lear through the medium of a symbolic system that orders identities according to titles and parts in the kingdom, and it addresses Lear according to the supreme title and part that is only questionably still his. Significantly, Gloucester's address to Lear takes the grammatical form of a question that implies the uncertainty of the identity it tries to ascertain—an uncertainty intensified by the question's negative construction. More radically, Gloucester's question implies the uncertainty of the very logic of titles and parts according to which who Lear is may be determined.

Lear's recovery is triggered in earnest, I claim, when he is faced with his sovereign identity not as fact but as question. Ironically, the enunciatory form of the question registers precisely the *reality* of Lear's situation in the kingdom—that is, the irreducible ambiguity of his political status. Lear replies to Gloucester's question first by affirming his correspondence to the title in question: "Ay, every inch a king./When I do stare, see how the subject quakes./I pardon that man's life. What was thy cause?/Adultery?" (4.6.106–9). Lear affirms here in full-blown, hyperbolic mode that he is indeed the king. What his answer implies is that the king is a part, among whose offices it is to act as judge, which he performs throughout this monologue while scripting parts for an imaginary kingdom of imaginary subjects like the adulterer and the apothecary, whom, at the end, he asks to give him "an ounce of civet . . . to/sweeten my imagination. There's money for thee" (4.6.126–7). Presumably, at this point, the actor playing Lear will be instructed to reach his hand out toward Gloucester. Blind Gloucester approaches or receives its touch when he cries, "O, let me kiss that hand!" (4.6.128–9). Remarkably, Gloucester's reply straddles the border between Lear's make-believe kingdom and one in which Gloucester would have ritualistically kissed his sovereign's hand. In reaching toward Lear, Gloucester may appear to Lear to play the part of apothecary, while his speech embeds this gesture in the role of a courtier.

When Lear answers, "Let me wipe it first, it smells of mortality" (4.6.128–9), he moves already closer toward reappearing in the world and responding to another beyond the imaginary kingdom he madly inhabits. He enters now into dialogue with Gloucester, who asks, "Dost thou know me?" (4.6.131). The answer will be delayed for another forty lines. Lear speaks first of eyes:

LEAR I remember thine eyes well enough. Dost thou
    squiny at me?
    No, do thy worst, blind Cupid, I'll not love.
    Read thou this challenge, mark but the penning of it.
GLOUCESTER Were all thy letters suns, I could not see one.
EDGAR [aside]
    I would not take this from report: it is,
    And my heart breaks at it.
LEAR Read.
GLOUCESTER What? With the case of eyes?
LEAR Oh ho, are you there with me? No eyes in your
    head, nor no money in your purse? Your eyes are in a
    heavy case, your purse in a light, yet you see how this
    world goes.
GLOUCESTER I see it feelingly.

(4.6.132–45)

This exchange is rife with irony and cruelty, and it synthesizes and reverberates with themes sounded earlier in the play. Lear cruelly mocks Gloucester for what he literally cannot do—see and read—and Gloucester's reply uncannily recalls and puns on what he figuratively could not do—read "letters" like "suns"/"sons." Lear's reference to "blind Cupid"—in Shakespeare's times, the sign at the door of a brothel (according to Benedick in

Much Ado about Nothing)—may allude to the adultery through which Gloucester sired Edmund, a theme Lear had already mentioned.[44] Mad Lear conjures up with unwitting precision the ghosts of his blind interlocutor's past. In this dialogue they revisit between them the prior misuse of eyes. As spectator of the exchange, Gloucester's misread son Edgar registers in his aside its sheer cruelty—a cruelty that woundingly opens up through the very site of the wound a way out of the framework of sovereign recognition.

In the derangement of the senses, sight gives way to touch—"I see it feelingly"—gives way to hearing. "Look with thine ears," Lear tells Gloucester before rehearsing, for the last time in the play, a scene of mock judgment, variations of which he has staged compulsively since his madness. Lear conjures up verbally a topsy-turvy kingdom in which justice trades places with criminality, and the distinction between virtue and vice slides according to whoever is entitled to the offices of power. For this realm, "[g]et thee glass eyes," he counsels, "And like a scurvy politician seem / To see the things thou dost not" (4.6.167–8). The kingdom he conjures up is a realm of misrecognition that mocks the one he presided over. In reflecting on the perversion of judgment, he "reviews," so to speak, the use and misuse of eyes.

Finally, Lear recognizes Gloucester in telling him:

If thou wilt weep my fortunes, take my eyes.
I know thee well enough, thy name is Gloucester.
Thou must be patient. We came crying hither:
Thou knowst the first time that we smell the air
We wawl and cry.

(4.6.172–6)

Lear's recognition takes place, it seems, in response to Gloucester's weeping and as an affirmation in general of the eyes' capacity to weep over their capacity to see. Indeed, it affirms the priority of weeping over seeing as the first thing we do—upon smelling the air—with our eyes. Lear recovers his senses and reappears to Gloucester, then, not as the king who sees but as the child who cries. His recovery is figured here as a rebirth into the world, a rebirth in which the cry doubly registers our alienation from others in the world as well as performs our first act of communication.

What kind of act, then, is the cry? And what kind of role is the child? The cry is an act that is original to speech but is not properly an act of speech. Without semantic content, it is an act of pure expressivity that communicates, precisely, "nothing." The cry is original but not anterior to or outside of speech; it inhabits speech as its ineradicable excess, marking the speechlessness constitutive of speech itself. The agent of the cry is the child, which figures, I propose, the part of having no title or part in the kingdom. It is by assuming this part of having no part that Lear refinds his senses sufficiently to recognize Gloucester and to reappear in the world.

Lear reflects on the modality of his reappearance in the world by means of a theatrical metaphor. "I will preach to thee," he tells Gloucester, "mark me":

GLOUCESTER   Alack, alack the day!
LEAR
　　When we are born we cry that we are come
　　To this great stage of fools.

　　　　　　　　　　　　　　　　　　　　(4.6.176–9)

To appear in the world as child is to appear as fool and among fools. From viewing the kingdom as a hierarchically articulated totality of characters with titles and parts, Lear now imagines the kingdom as an anarchic stage on which all characters play the part of having no part. Immediately after this pronouncement, he madly shifts to another scenario—

　　　　　　　This a good block:
　　It were a delicate stratagem to shoe
　　A troop of horse with felt. I'll put it in proof
　　And when I have stolen upon these son-in-laws,
　　Then kill, kill, kill, kill, kill, kill!

　　　　　　　　　　　　　　　　　　　　(4.6.179–83)

—and interrupts the process of his own rebirth. Lear's recovery does not take place punctually but in fits and starts. And there is the question of whether he ever fully recovers at all. In act 4, scene 7 Lear wakes from his sleep to recognize Cordelia—but strikingly not Kent who, in or out of his guise as Caius, stands beside her in her tent, along with an attending gentleman, all of them awaiting Lear's awakening. What accounts for Lear's recognition of Cordelia? And what accounts for the selectivity of his recognition, the partiality of his return to the world?

Upon waking, Lear takes Cordelia first to be "a spirit," asking her, "where did you die?" (4.7.49). Thinking himself to be dead, utterly confused as to his whereabouts, he tests his condition by pricking himself with a sharp object. Seeing Cordelia kneel, he kneels too and gradually articulates his recognition of her in the following speech:

> Pray do not mock me.
> I am a very foolish, fond old man,
> Fourscore and upward, not an hour more nor less;
> And to deal plainly,
> I fear I am not in my perfect mind.
> Methinks I should know you and know this man,
> Yet I am doubtful; for I am mainly ignorant
> What place this is and all the skill I have
> Remembers not these garments; nor I know not
> Where I did lodge last night. Do not laugh at me,
> For, as I am a man, I think this lady
> To be my child Cordelia.
>
> (4.7.59–69)

Cavell notes of these last three lines that Lear recognizes himself first before he recognizes Cordelia: his allowing himself to be recognized, to be revealed to another, serves as condition for his recognition of the other. In this aspect of self-revelation, these last three lines repeat and extend the self-revelation at the beginning of the speech: "Pray do not mock me. . . ." They hark back also to Gloucester's structurally similar revelation of himself before his recognition of Edgar's innocence: "O my follies! Then Edgar was abused./Kind gods, forgive me that, and prosper him!"

In these resonant instances, the play's fathers expose themselves as fallible, culpable, and vulnerable to shame in belated recognition of the children they had banished. "I know you do not love me," Lear tells Cordelia, "for your sisters/Have, as I do remember, done me wrong./You have some cause, they have not" (4.7.73–5). Echoing the first scene of the play, Lear speaks again of his daughters' love for him, their father. Echoing the first scene, Cordelia says again, "No cause, no cause," with "cause" constituting a Latinate substitute for the Anglo-Saxon "thing."[45] Once again, when Lear speaks of love, Cordelia says "nothing."

What has changed here in this father's recognition of his child, in this reconciliation that so resonates with the earlier scene that resulted in banishment? I suggest that the play restages as questions: What is a father? And what is a child? In the earlier scene, "father" names the title and part of supreme authority in the household—which, being the royal household, implies the king's paternal authority over the state. The "child" figures as extension and function of the father's will, in short, as his heir, through which the authority of the father perpetuates itself even after his death, when he is no longer part of the kingdom, or in Lear's case, after his abdication has effectively situated him outside the kingdom in what Lacan calls the zone "between two deaths." The child is imperceptible outside this framework, visible and audible only to the extent that she plays the part necessary for constituting the kingdom as a finite, bordered entity that can, like a substance, be divided and disposed of, that can be *had* and transmitted as property.

In saying "nothing," Cordelia refuses to play her designated part and deviates from the role of child as heir. Her "nothing" challenges the topology whereby the kingdom can be constituted as whole, in relation to which Lear conceives of freedom as end outside of political life. Her "nothing" exposes the irreducibility of the human being to his or her identification according to title and part,, and performs an act of love in revealing the gap that keeps love for another from being collapsed with loving another as father, king, or lord. "Nothing" interrupts the logic whereby the political realm is conceived of as sovereign totality of parts. From the perspective of the political realm so conceived, "nothing" registers as silence or caesura. Cordelia is the child who acts beyond the act to introduce such *infancy* into the political realm. In so doing, she enacts a different conception of what a child is—that is, the child as newcomer in the world who is capable of putting into motion a new beginning with the unpredictable consequences that genuine action implies.

The fact of generation—spoken of with pronounced horror by Lear, Gloucester, and finally also Edgar—ensure that the world is and always will be incomplete, its horizon open, its future unpredictable. The conception of child as heir is at odds with the capacity of child as newcomer. The former attempts to stabilize the fact of generation and subsume it to a predictable patrilineal system of succession wherein each successive generation— conceived of as *next* rather than *new*—cyclically repeats and replaces the last. Even rebellion or revolt against the existing order may participate finally in the conservative logic of child as heir, to the extent that the dissatisfied or usurping rebel becomes the *next* placeholder who replaces the last placeholder instead of initiating something new in the world.

Among the children in the play, it is Cordelia alone who departs from the pattern of child as heir to act in the non-role of child as newcomer— non-role because this child has, by definition, no title or part in the kingdom. Her speech and action in this capacity are radically unscripted, unconditioned: mute or infant from the perspective of the kingdom. In contrast, her sisters perform the part of child as heir to murderous extent, in conspiracy with their mutual paramour, Edmund, both victim and proponent of the kingdom's patterns of inheritance. Even Edgar, bent on revenge and reclaiming his title as Gloucester's heir, remains locked in the patriarchal conception of the child, attached to the given image of himself as displaced and rightful heir.

What happens, then, when Lear awakens to recognize the child he had banished, the child he now distinguishes from her sisters who, wanting his place, flattered him and did him wrong? What kind of father recognizes what kind of child? Significantly, the father is, in Cordelia's formulation, a "child-changed father" (4.7.17). It is as "child-changed father" that Lear awakens to see attending his rebirth to the world a woman, a man, and a "Gentleman" that in the 1608 Quarto is called "Doctor." Of the couple, Lear thinks he should "know you and know this man / Yet I am doubtful; for I am mainly ignorant / What place this is" (4.7.54–6). Hesitantly, he proceeds from ignorance to knowledge in addressing to his audience a tentative gesture in need of responsive acknowledgment from the other: "Do not laugh at me, / For, as I am a man, I think this lady / To be my child Cordelia." To which Cordelia replies, "And so I am, I am" (4.7.70). Lear thus reappears to the world by addressing and entering into conversation with another, a conversation in which who he is and who the other is are not already determined but depend for their disclosure on the process of the subjects' unconditioned interaction with each other. The "child-changed father" assumes aspects of the child as newcomer.

If in this scene Lear proceeds from ignorance to knowledge in keeping with the classic Aristotelian definition of tragic recognition, the knowledge he arrives at is not simply the reversal or overcoming of ignorance, as if knowledge and ignorance were symmetrical opposites of each other. Rather, the play shows Lear, in his approach to Cordelia, not already knowing who or what the other is but not knowing as well who or what he is. The "child-changed father" acknowledges the separateness of the child at the same time that he acknowledges his own separateness in the world they share between them. Lear does not assert his status as knowing but is shown engaged in a process of *re-cognition* in which the very possibility of knowing involves necessary exposure of and passage through not-knowing.[46]

Along with the appearance of Lear as "child-changed father" in the play there emerges the figure most strikingly occluded throughout, the figure empirically absent and evoked on multiple levels with distrust and suspicion:

the figure of the mother.[47] From the perspective of the kingdom in its patriarchal articulation, the mother is the agent of generation potentially at odds with patrilineal succession, the partner of a conception that splits the subject of conception as understanding. "I cannot conceive you," Kent tells Gloucester at the very beginning of the play. "Sir, this young fellow's mother could," Gloucester punningly replies (1.1.11–2). From the perspective of the kingdom, the mother must—like the child as newcomer—be suppressed to stabilize the conception of the child as heir. In relation to the "child-changed father," then, Cordelia appears to him as the "child-changed mother."

What does the "child-changed mother" do? She helps Lear make a new beginning in the world. It is impossible for a newcomer to make an absolutely new beginning in the world that is not always already dependent on the fundamental condition of human plurality. The beginning a newcomer makes is one that constitutes entry into an existing human world. His capacity to act may be compromised by his assimilation into a given script that dictates his title and part, *what* he is. Or he may through his capacity to act disclose who he uniquely is in interaction with others. Cordelia helps Lear make a new beginning by forgiving him and thus undoing the consequences of his mistakes and his banishment of her, opening up the possibility of an undetermined future. She forgives him by saying again "nothing" in inflected form: "No cause, no cause." By saying "nothing," Cordelia had precisely performed her injunction, "Love, and be silent," and let their love be registered in court as a caesura that keeps her love for Lear as *whatever* from being collapsed with love for him according to his title as master. By saying "No cause, no cause" in reply to his admission of culpability, his remark that she has some cause *not* to love him, Cordelia responds with forgiveness as gift that cancels the economy of guilt and indebtedness and separates love from the causal chain that reacts to the event of banishment.[48]

But what kind of new beginning does Lear make? How is it that he recognizes Cordelia but not Kent next to her, thinking him perhaps to be her husband, as his question, "Am I in France?" (4.7.76) suggests? Lear's recovery of his senses and return to the world is a circumscribed one that takes Cordelia as its central reference point. He is indeed belatedly putting into action the thought he expressed in act 1, scene 1, that he would set his rest on "her kind nursery" (1.1.124). Lear as "child-changed father" relates to Cordelia as "child-changed mother" by entering into conversation with her as one who acknowledges his own fundamental dependence on another or even others for the disclosure of who he is. While Lear shows his awareness

of the blindness inherent in his seeing, what he remains blind to is the blindness in the seeing of the (m)other, which makes her necessarily also incomplete, radically dependent on and essentially exposed to a world that is
plural, multiple—beyond two—for the disclosure of who she is.

Thus, taken prisoner by Edmund and his men, Lear imagines and
embraces a captivity that would isolate Cordelia and himself from others:

> Come, let's away to prison;
> We two alone will sing like birds i'the cage.
> When thou dost ask me blessing I'll kneel down
> And ask of thee forgiveness. So we'll live
> And pray, and sing, and tell old tales, and laugh
> At gilded butterflies, and hear poor rogues
> Talk of court news; and we'll talk with them too—
> Who loses and who wins, who's in, who's out—
> And take upon's the mystery of things
> As if we were God's spies. And we'll wear out
> In a walled prison packs and sects of great ones
> That ebb and flow by the moon.

$$(5.3.8–19)$$

Ironically, Shakespeare makes the space of the prison in Lear's fantasy a space
of freedom and happiness, underlining the problematic character of the pri-
vacy Lear presents. If in act 1, scene 1 Lear's conception of freedom entailed
an opposition to the political realm, here he again sets up the topological
opposition between freedom and happiness, on the one hand, and the kingdom, on the other. He situates freedom and happiness outside of a world
lived between and among a plurality of human beings. In this way, he mir-
rors and endorses the logic of his captors, who wield the juridical-political
instrument of imprisonment as Lear once did that of banishment. This
speech shows ironically the automatism of a political machine whereby the
main actors destroy the very kingdom they fight to possess.

While the play shows Lear's rhapsodic embrace of captivity as the enclo-
sure of a world of "we two alone," it shows at the same time Cordelia's
response to the situation:

> For thee, oppressed King, I am cast down;
> Myself could else outfrown false fortune's frown.
> Shall we not see these daughters and these sisters?

$$(5.3.5–7)$$

To this proposal Lear objects and retreats: "No, no, no, no" (5.3.8). In these lines (her last words in the play), Cordelia shows again her coldly lucid and unsentimental tendency to rationalize roles that she displayed in act 1, scene 1, when she spoke of loving "your majesty / According to my bond, no more nor less" (1.1.92–3). She reiterates here—and again Lear does not hear—that she inhabits the world by playing more than a part in relation to Lear. She insists on the singularity of her destiny, implicated with but separate from his, and on how she potentially "could else outfrown false fortune's frown." It is by insisting on this separateness that she, paradoxically, shows her solidarity with Lear and her openness to a world in which she must play more than one part but that does not end with the sum of these parts.

The Framing and Wounding of Spectatorship

I discuss in this section the significance of Edgar's emergence as choric figure or surrogate spectator in the second half of the play. Edgar figures as the character who *sees for* the reader and the audience, the one whose multiple disguises allow him to serve as a framing agent in relation to the other characters. At the same time as Edgar comments in soliloquies and asides on the sufferings of Lear and Gloucester, he becomes the protagonist of the subplot become revenge tragedy, defeating Edmund at the end and even, it is implied, succeeding Lear as survivor-king. If the Quarto version includes Edgar along with Lear in the play's title, the Folio attributes the very last lines of the play to him—

> The weight of this sad time we must obey,
> Speak what we feel, not what we ought to say.
> The oldest hath borne most; we that are young
> Shall never see so much, nor live so long.

> (5.3.322–5)

—giving him the task of formulating what it is to have seen King Lear as well as, implicitly, raising for the audience the question of what it is to have seen *King Lear*.

As privileged spectator in the play, Edgar functions as *framing agent* in more than one sense of the verb "to frame"—both structuring the experience of the reader or audience as well as deceiving and serving as trap for the audience's gaze. It is precisely by making the audience fall for this trap, I claim, that the play uncannily involves us in suffering a dramatic losing and refinding of our senses and opens up the possibility of a reorientation in the world.

Edgar comments on the plights of Lear and Gloucester and begins doing so, significantly, after the former has gone mad and the latter blind—that is, after the fathers have respectively lost their sense(s). After the episode on the heath, the second half of the play shows us the ordeals of the mad and the blind, and shows them through the mediation of one who plays the part of being mad but, through playing this part, assures us that he is neither mad nor blind. As the characters lose their senses and the kingdom devolves into civil war, Edgar serves effectively to restore a guiding perspective on the kingdom.

He delivers his first soliloquy on seeing Lear's suffering after he has played in the mock trial Lear stages of his daughters on Gloucester's premises after leaving the heath. Right after Kent and the Fool escort Lear away, Edgar sheds his Poor Tom disguise to speak in propria persona, confiding his response to the audience:

> When we our betters see bearing our woes,
> We scarcely think our miseries our foes.
> Who alone suffers, suffers most i'the mind,
> Leaving free things and happy shows behind.
> But then the mind much sufferance doth o'erskip,
> When grief hath mates and bearing fellowship.
> How light and portable my pain seems now,
> When that which makes me bend makes the King bow,
> He childed as I fathered.
>
> (3.6.99–107)

The passage reflects on what it is to be a spectator of tragedy, beginning with an allusion to the genre's classic concern with the suffering of the high-born. By using the first-person plural, Edgar speaks not just for himself but for members of the audience who are supposedly linked with him in fellowship in seeing the suffering of "our betters," who bear "our woes" in our stead. Seeing those hierarchically above one suffer lightens the pain of the tragic spectator, who has relatively less distance to fall. The speech pivots around the chiasmic "He childed as I fathered," which makes explicit the underlying comparison Edgar has been making between Lear as protagonist and himself as spectator. Tragic spectatorship, the speech underlines, depends on the operations of identification and parallelism. Around the chiasmus the speech turns to the particular circumstances of this speaker, whose status as spectator entails his assuming a persona:

> Tom, away;
> Mark the high noises, and thyself bewray
> When false opinion, whose wrong thoughts defile thee,
> In thy just proof repeals and reconciles thee.
>
> (3.6.107–10)

Edgar speaks of how he must adopt disguise to remain in the kingdom but not appear to others while his true identity is defiled by "false opinion." He will patiently defer exposure of himself to others, whom he can thus watch from a position parallel to that of the reader outside the text or the tragic spectator on the other side of the stage.

A question that persistently baffles readers and the audience is why Edgar remains in this position of non-exposure in relation to Gloucester after the latter has realized that Edgar is indeed innocent, and has even pronounced in Edgar's presence, "O dear son Edgar, / The food of thy abused father's wrath, / Might I but live to see thee in my touch, / I'd say I had eyes again" (4.1.23–6). Edgar only exposes himself to Gloucester when he is armed and ready to fight Edmund, and to the other characters when he has defeated Edmund and reclaimed his title. Upon hearing his father speak of wanting to see him in his touch again, Edgar comments aside:

> O gods! Who is't can say "I am at the worst"?
> I am worse than e'er I was . . .
> And worse I may be yet; the worst is not
> So long as we can say "This is the worst."
>
> (4.1.27–30)

Edgar keeps to the sidelines and preserves the distance between his own suffering and the suffering of others, taking solace, paradoxically, in the capacity to observe periodically of the spectacle he watches that "[t]his is the worst." He endures patiently amid suffering while repeatedly counseling Gloucester likewise to endure—counsel that seems to be implicitly extended to the play's reader and audience as well.

Edgar figures in the play, of course, doubly as spectator and actor—as do all the other characters in the kingdom. What distinguishes Edgar is how he maintains more than the other characters a strict separation between being a spectator and being an actor. This proposal may sound at first counterintuitive, since Edgar's very status as non-exposed spectator depends, on a pragmatic level, on his playing various parts in the kingdom. These disguises serve, however, to sustain a more fundamental opposition for him between acting and viewing. Before his banishment, at the beginning of the play, Edgar is a naïf who does not question the "naturalness" of his received title and part in the kingdom as heir of Gloucester. He accepts as given the customs and laws whereby he is deemed legitimate and his half brother a bastard. Like his father, this naïf succumbs easily to Edmund's plot. It is only after being deceived and banished from the kingdom that Edgar begins to inhabit the world critically, to question rather than readily accept appearances, and himself to manipulate them. The play allegorizes this new critical stance in *theatrical* terms: banished Edgar develops a distinctly theatrical relationship to the kingdom.

In his banishment, Edgar becomes the veritable double of his bastard brother, Edmund, beholding the kingdom from a position of externality and conspiring for membership in the kingdom precisely from this external position. Edmund, in his plot of usurpation, wanted Edgar's place in the kingdom as successor to Gloucester. Having become de jure "Gloucester," Edmund does not stop but puts himself on track to becoming, through Goneril or Regan, the next king. Edgar, in a counterplot of revenge and restitution, wants his place back in the kingdom as Gloucester's heir. Ironically, the play shows how he may indeed finally become the next king, thus doubling all the way to the end his bastard brother's ambition.

If Edmund grounds and legitimates his conspiracy of usurpation in the name of a "nature" he deems outside and prior to the juridical-political order, Edgar legitimates his plot for vengeance in the name of a formal justice aligned with truth that is likewise situated outside the political realm become a sphere of "false opinion." While "false opinion" prevails in the kingdom, Edgar will not reappear, no matter who it is that may solicit his reappearance. He will reappear among others as nothing other than heir of Gloucester, the title and part he finds rightfully his as articulated within the framework of patrilineal succession. That, for Edgar, is his *true* identity and determines what it is for him—beyond the series of disguises—*truly* to be an actor in the kingdom.

Edgar is unwaveringly directed toward reclaiming his title and part. To the determination of his identity as such he remains throughout nostalgically attached; this attachment orients his trajectory and informs his principle of non-exposure to others. He views the kingdom and its members, then, as means toward his end of restitution. In theatrical terms, Edgar views the kingdom spectatorially as a stage that awaits his return and vindication, a stage on which he may at last heroically reappear as actor to purge and be purged of "false opinion." Ironically, the kingdom in which he would reinstall himself—the framework that articulates his title and part—has collapsed by the end of the play. While he may win the "repeal and reconciliation" he aims for, there are few left who can give substance to his purely formal victory.

Edgar's emergence as privileged spectator in the second half of *King Lear* is, I argue, a highly problematic development inscribed in a cycle of tragic repetition rather than one that opens up the possibility of a new political future. Revenge, after all, simply reenacts—by *reacting to*—the very logic whereby the one seeking redress was wounded in the first place. As Edmund viewed Edgar and Gloucester as nothing more than the bearers of the titles and parts he wants, reducing them to nothing more than types or characters in the political realm, so too did Gloucester view his sons only according to their identities as articulated in juridical-political terms—that is, as nothing more or less than legitimate and illegitimate. In so doing, both deny the humanity of the other, displaying blindness to the singularity of the human being as an actor always in excess of given title or part.

Edgar is the victim of this intergenerational blindness—a blindness that is, however, not limited to this family, but that also structures the parallel fate of Cordelia, the play's other banished child, in the royal household. Whereas Cordelia opens up a new possibility beyond the cycle of tragic repetition, Edgar repeats the familial pattern precisely in remaining nostalgically and narcissistically attached to the image of himself as "nothing" if not heir of Gloucester—"poor Tom. / That's something yet; Edgar I nothing am"— and to the kingdom as a space of appearances, call it a stage, wherein he may find his "true" image reflected back to him.

It is his attachment to his "true" image, to which he has a quasi-proprietorial relationship, that keeps him from exposing himself to others, even his father, who repeatedly expresses the desire to "see" Edgar again in his touch before he dies. I examine one particular occasion in which Edgar ignores this appeal and postpones self-exposure. On the top of Dover Cliff, a suicidal Gloucester cries out before jumping, "If Edgar live, O, bless him!" (4.6.40). At this moment, instead of intervening to relieve Gloucester of his suicidal despair, Edgar lets him fall. Of course, what we find—not immediately but after initial shock and incomprehension—in this exceedingly bizarre scene is that, while Gloucester may fall, *there is no cliff*. In other words, the cliff Gloucester falls over is one conjured up verbally by Edgar, who, staging Gloucester's suicide in this scene, takes on the function of surrogate playwright or director in addition to that of surrogate spectator. It is through this scene above all, I propose, that Shakespeare's play raises for the reader and audience the question of what it is to be a spectator of the tragedy and differentiates itself from Edgar's performance of his answer to the question.

Blind Gloucester has asked Edgar, disguised as Poor Tom, to lead him to the edge of Dover Cliff, telling him suggestively as they set off, "From that place / I shall no leading need" (4.1.80–1). Why Dover? Gloucester is ostensibly following Lear there. Lear has been escorted to Dover to meet Cordelia, whose arrival with her forces from France is first mentioned by Kent in act 3, scene 1, when he asks an emissary knight to ride there to meet her. Indeed, all the characters will eventually make their way to Dover, except for the Fool, who was last seen in the company of Lear and Kent setting out for Dover but who disappears for unexplained reasons from the play. Dover marks, then, the final destination for the characters in the kingdom: it will be the terminus of the lives of most of the characters, and it will serve as the scene of the play's denouement. Geographically as well as politically, Dover is the very bourne of Britain, the kingdom's closest point to France and the Continent. In multiple ways, then, Dover figures in the play the principle of the limit. The limit Gloucester intends to cross there is that between life and death.

At Dover Cliff—if the scene can actually be placed there—Edgar stages Gloucester's suicide. Just when Gloucester is beginning to question the reliability of his guide, Edgar gives him a detailed description of the view from the top of the cliff:

> Come on, sir, here's the place. Stand still: how fearful
> And dizzy 'tis to cast one's eyes so low.
> The crows and choughs that wing the midway air
> Show scarce so gross as beetles. Half-way down
> Hangs one that gathers samphire, dreadful trade;
> Methinks he seems no bigger than his head.
> The fishermen that walk upon the beach
> Appear like mice, and yon tall anchoring barque
> Diminished to her cock, her cock a buoy
> Almost too small for sight. The murmuring surge
> That on th'unnumbered idle pebble chafes,
> Cannot be heard so high. I'll look no more,
> Lest my brain turn and the deficient sight
> Topple down headlong.

(4.6.11–24)

This description convinces Gloucester that he has arrived at the end of his journey. He asks to be led to the edge of the cliff, and he falls—but not over the cliff, it turns out. He faints and, when he revives, Edgar addresses him no longer in the guise of Poor Tom but as an anonymous peasant passerby, who marvels at Gloucester's survival of such a fall and describes to him the figure of Poor Tom as a fiend from whom Gloucester should feel himself lucky to have been saved. At the end of this complex production, Edgar tells Gloucester, "Bear free and patient thoughts" (4.6.79).

What the play shows here is, in effect, a play within the play. Edgar's staging of Gloucester's fall over Dover Cliff and subsequent revival has been interpreted in terms of an exorcism—of Poor Tom as fiendish proponent of suicide. This micro-drama can also be read as a miniature tragedy, which like exorcism aims for the effect of purification or catharsis.

In asides to the audience, Edgar discloses his dramaturgical intentions in staging his father's suicide. Before Gloucester's fall, he remarks, "Why I do trifle thus with his despair/Is done to cure it" (4.6.33–4). He professes, then, a therapeutic purpose resonant with the Aristotelian definition of tragedy as "arousing pity and fear, wherewith to accomplish its catharsis of such emotions" (6.27–8.1449b). He acknowledges the risk of such a cure—that is, that it could kill—when, standing over Gloucester's unconscious body, he wonders: "And yet I know not how conceit may rob/The treasury of life when life itself/Yields to the theft/. . ./Thus might he pass indeed. Yet he revives" (4.6.42–4, 47). Gloucester indeed does not die but awakens to be congratulated by Edgar as passerby upon his miraculous survival. He will, however, return to desperate thoughts again when he hears of the capture of Lear and Cordelia: "No further, sir; a man may rot even here," he says (5.2.8). Edgar has not cured Gloucester of his despair but, extending his biological life, only extended his life-as-despair. The cure Edgar offers works practically, then, as a placebo, which masks symptoms of the affliction but misses its underlying etiological structure. This placebo functions as substitute for another cure that presents itself as a perhaps more effective— certainly, for Gloucester, more desirable—option: Edgar's revelation of his identity.

Instead of stepping in to relieve Gloucester's pain by exposing himself, Edgar abets his father's plan to end his pain by "renouncing the world." He leaves his father's sense of the world intact by refusing to enter it as a world potentially *between* them. The play shows Edgar preferring to relate to his father *theatrically*, treating Gloucester as if he were a figure on stage, in relation to which Edgar himself would be situated before, like a member of the audience, or behind, like a playwright or director. Maintaining a strict divide between being an actor *or* a spectator/playwright, Edgar keeps his own sense of what it is to act in the world—his own *agenda*, so to speak—intact and separate from the pain and suffering of the other.

Edgar defers exposing himself to others for the sake of an agenda oriented toward his reappearance as avenging hero in the kingdom, poised to reclaim the name he finds rightfully his. He views the present scene not as present, withholding his presence in it, but from the vantage point of a future restitution that organizes his relationship to the present. That future restitution evokes not only the object of a lost identity but depends nostalgically also on the framework of a phantom kingdom—"phantom" because the kingdom that would articulate the relationship between Gloucester and Edgar as father and heir, consecutive bearers of the same name, is already in ruins. The Gloucester before Edgar is, like himself, an exile, dispossessed of his title and part in the kingdom, no longer "Gloucester." The Gloucester who wishes to "see" his son again is disjunct from the Gloucester who bears the paternal name Edgar wishes to succeed. This disjunction motivates Edgar's deferral of exposure to Gloucester until he is armed and ready to fight Edmund and can thus address his father as the father whose title and part he fights for.

Privileging an envisioned end, Edgar treats the present as a "meantime," counseling "patience and endurance," "the ripeness is all," and so forth, to a Gloucester to whom he relates theatrically—as spectator through disguises and as playwright-director in staging his therapeutic suicide. His dramaturgical success in the latter turns on his description of the view from Dover Cliff, which effectively dupes Gloucester but also, notoriously, the reader and the audience. Edgar's detailed description of this view creates a verbal picture organized, as critics Jonathan Goldberg and Christopher Pye have analyzed, according to early modern principles of perspectival representation formalized most famously by Alberti and Dürer.[49] The description assumes and appeals to a punctiform viewing subject in relation to the space it maps out from the abyssal foreground to the sea in the background, with the buoy marking the picture's vanishing point. The description successfully addresses and dupes Gloucester. And it successfully addresses and dupes the reader or spectator as well.

Gloucester falls over the cliff Edgar represents for his imagination at the very moment the character in the text or the actor on stage falls over the cliff the play represents for our imagination. Gloucester gets up after his fall and remains an unwitting actor in the rest of Edgar's production. After recovering from the initial shock and confusion, the reader or spectator catches on to Edgar's asides and realizes what Gloucester does not know—that there was no cliff, and that he is acting in a play (within the play). The play establishes in this scene the reader or audience's maximal complicity with Edgar as surrogate spectator, a complicity that follows paradoxically, however, our being duped like Gloucester and falling into the play, crossing the limit whereby we assume ourselves to be safely and wholly *external to* the play.

We fall with Gloucester then. On a simplistic level, we may think that what this fall does is suddenly remind us *that* we are watching a play or reading a work of literature. The thud the falling body makes reminds us that the surface it falls on is not sand or soil but stage. The play thus interrupts its own power of absorbing us in its illusion and jolts us out of our supposed passivity as viewers. But the moment of Gloucester's fall does more than just issue the banal reminder that we are watching a play, which would simply reinforce our complicity with Edgar as distanced spectator within the play. Rather, this moment raises the question of *how* we are watching the play in a way that interrupts our very complicity with Edgar and goes beyond the logic of spectatorship staked on this complicity.

In falling with Gloucester, we are like him duped by Edgar's seeing *for us* the view from Dover Cliff. In accepting Edgar as the representative of our seeing and the view given us in the verbal picture, we are, parallel to Gloucester, deprived of sight. In relation to this privation, Edgar's description serves a restorative function: it allows Gloucester and the audience to "see" in the absence of sight, establishing in the "mind's eye" a reconstructible, imaginable picture. The picture given, organized according to the laws of geometral optics around a unitary point of view, is precisely an image that can be reconstructed by the blind; the space of vision it maps out can be represented, made present again, to the mind's eye. Edgar's description addresses the seeing subject qua thinking subject in a way that aligns the experience of vision with the activity of cognition. In seeing after and *like* Edgar, we (along with Gloucester) think we *know* what we are given to see. Precisely in thinking we know what we see, we are duped into falling.

In the surprise of falling with Gloucester, then, the play stages for us an uncanny encounter with the blindness of our own gaze—the blindness that inhabits, paradoxically, our seeing-as-knowing. Like the anamorphic skull that Hans Holbein places as a memento mori in the foreground of his 1533 painting *The Ambassadors*, which disrupts and shows the picture's privileging otherwise of a unitary point of view, Gloucester's fall occasions a displacement from our position as spectators capable of comprehending the events of the tragedy from a distanced, external vantage point.[50] The event of Gloucester's fall interrupts our fascination with the picture Edgar presents to us, which reflects back to us our capacity to *know*. This picture "frames" our spectatorship by both soliciting and structuring our seeing as well as screening our access to the drama taking place, which emerges only belatedly to our understanding. The play shows how our relationship to this picture constitutes a misrecognition, opening up a gap between the sense of sight and sense as intelligible meaning, involving us thereby in a dramatic losing and refinding of our senses.

Gloucester's fall enacts vis-à-vis the audience, I propose, the event of Cordelia's "nothing." Through Gloucester's fall, the play stages an act beyond the act that opens up the boundaries of its own theater of sovereignty, exposing us to its own incompleteness and to the incompleteness of our seeing. Specifically, it does so by staging an act beyond the act in excess of the theater of sovereignty that Edgar, following other characters in the play, preeminently Lear, stages in situating himself vis-à-vis the kingdom as sovereign totality. Gloucester's fall constitutes an event whose meaning cannot be stabilized in confirmation of any one or anyone's perspective on the whole or image of oneself as would-be part of a phantom whole. Gloucester's fall constitutes, precisely, an event that is improper, unassimilable to any existing program or agenda for the future that would deny the contingency of the future by rendering it predictable in conformity with the rules governing the existing order. Through this event, the play performs a wounding of the spectator qua sovereign spectator topologically external to the play, in a way evocative of how Cordelia's "nothing" opens up the limits of Lear's kingdom as a totality of titles and parts that guarantees his end of freedom.

In so doing, the play raises the question of what it is to see *King Lear* beyond the answer it seems to provide through the elevation of one of its characters, Edgar, as model spectator. In setting up Edgar as guiding consciousness in its second half, the play creates for the spectator a double in the theater, then problematizes this relationship by showing how the double's position of sympathetic externality to others in the kingdom merely perpetuates the logic whereby he was excluded from the kingdom in the first place. In this problematization, Shakespeare's play displays a shattering cruelty toward the false hopes and false cures offered by characters who remain trapped in the cycle of tragic repetition, looking upon themselves and each other *theatrically* as characters or types in a kingdom. "An end to master-pieces," Antonin Artaud cries against Shakespeare in his manifesto against a theater that since the Renaissance has situated "the spectacle on one side and the audience on the other."[51] Ante and contra Artaud, *King Lear* addresses the spectator in a wounding event that opens up that divide.

Towards a New Theatrum Mundi

The play's final scene, act 5, scene 3, is a long and complex dramatic con-struction framed by the capture of Lear and Cordelia at the beginning and the death of Lear at the end. It is strikingly marked by the absence of Lear in the middle as protagonist of the tragedy. Significantly, Lear disappears from the consciousness of the audience and the other characters, whose multiple conflicts over power occupy the middle and the foreground of the scene. Goneril and Regan fight first onstage over Edmund, then poison and stab each other offstage over him. Albany accuses Edmund of treason and adultery. A masked and armed Edgar returns to duel Edmund, then reveals his identity and reports the story of his ordeal in exile, including the news of Gloucester's dying upon learning of Edgar's identity.

It is only when Kent returns to inquire after the King that those on stage finally think again of Lear. "Great thing of us forgot!" Albany cries, speaking for the characters as well as the audience (5.3.535). The dying Edmund means at last to do some good and sends an emissary to stop Cordelia's hanging in prison. But it is too late. Lear reappears carrying Cordelia's dead body, then dies over it, with the three remaining characters—Albany, Kent, and Edgar—forming a chorus that comments on the sight. In the coda after Lear's death, Albany, the highest-ranking survivor, relinquishes the respon-sibility of ruling and tells Kent and Edgar, "Friends of my soul, you twain,/ Rule in this realm and the gored state sustain" (5.3.318–9). Kent declines, and Edgar emerges as the next king by default.

I schematize the construction of this scene to highlight how, in its middle parts, the subplot become revenge tragedy takes over the foreground of the play and displaces to the background Lear's status as protagonist and his story as central focus of the play. Edgar's ascendancy as hero of a revenge tragedy and his reappearance to others in the kingdom effectively eclipse what hap-pens to Lear and Cordelia in prison, *screening* for the reader and the audience the event of Cordelia's death. Preoccupied by what happens in the fore-ground, we too "the great thing" forget. The play reminds us cruelly, how-ever, of our forgetting.

I conclude my reading of *King Lear* by considering: What is at stake in our forgetting? And what is at stake in the play's cruel reminder? How is it that we could have forgotten the King? When he is taken away at the beginning of the scene, Lear has relapsed into madness and will not verily recover before his death. No longer master of his senses, he is also no longer master of the kingdom. The multiplicity of conflicts staged in this final scene bespeaks the fractured state of the kingdom and the absence therein of a center of command. In dramaturgical terms, act 5, scene 3 would appear to be the inverse of act 1, scene 1. Again, almost all the characters in the play are assembled in one place. But while in act 1 they form a unified audience in relation to Lear as sovereign focal point, in act 5 they are shown anarchically engaged in their own local struggles. These local struggles remain nevertheless structured by an idea of the center, since they can be described either as struggles for the position of sovereignty in the kingdom (Goneril, Regan, and Edmund) or efforts to make right the disjointed kingdom, according to some presupposition as to its proper framework (Albany, Kent, and Edgar). It is as principal proponent of the latter that Edgar finally reappears in the kingdom and claims the attention of the other characters and the audience as the play's focal point.

As the character who speaks the most number of lines after Lear in the play and whose private thoughts are conveyed more than any other character's to the reader or audience, Edgar is poised to elicit our sympathy. But, again and again, the play throws this sympathy into question, interrupting our complicity with this mediating figure and the logic of recognition he represents. We watch him defeat Edmund and reveal himself by reclaiming his name and rightful membership in the kingdom:

> I am no less in blood than thou art, Edmund;
> If more, the more thou'st wronged me.
> My name is Edgar and thy father's son.
> The gods are just and of our pleasant vices
> Make instruments to plague us:
> The dark and vicious place where thee he got
> Cost him his eyes.
>
> (5.3.165–71)

The defeated Edmund recognizes the victor and affirms his sense of justice: "Thou'st spoken right, 'tis true. / The wheel is come full circle, I am here" (5.3.171–2). And Albany likewise recognizes Edgar according to his restored title and part: "Methought thy very gait did prophesy / A royal nobleness. I must embrace thee" (5.3.173–4). Edgar has won the "repeal and reconciliation" he sought, but what promise for the future does his vindication bring?

As I mentioned above, there are few left in the kingdom who can participate in his purely formal victory. His efforts to right the kingdom, and to achieve the recognition of his rightful place in it end up ironically contributing to the general destruction in the kingdom. In his quest for restitution, Edgar slays Oswald and Edmund; the telling of his story effectively kills Gloucester, and its retelling screens the death of Cordelia. This apparently sympathetic character is, in practice, the equal or superior of Edmund, Goneril, Regan, and Cornwall in destructiveness. If these other characters usurp, maim, and murder in the name of "nature" or nihilistically without any attempt at justification whatsoever, Edgar too treats human life as expedient but does so in the name of justice.

At the beginning of the play, Lear and Gloucester had each banished one of their children to stabilize the kingdom as a framework in which the place of self and other in relation to the kingdom is already known. Here, one of these banished children reconstitutes through his act of vengeance the theater of sovereignty in which the actor who performs such an act can be recognized and known again. The future that Edgar's vindication promises is one that remains chained to the past, caught in an Oedipal cycle of repetition in which the animus of son against father ends up establishing the son in the position of the father within a predictable pattern of succession. Unwittingly, while watching his successor, seduced by the hope for a better future his vindication seems to offer, we forget the old King.

The reminder the play delivers is a shocking one—such a shock that Dr. Johnson could not read beyond this point, returning to the rest of the play only in his capacity as editor. The reappearance of Lear with Cordelia's dead body undercuts whatever hopefulness Edmund's victory may have offered. Still not quite in his "perfect mind," Lear cannot determine whether Cordelia is alive or dead, as he cannot quite care whether Kent may also have been Caius. Cordelia is the sole reference point of his world, and it is to her still that he looks to confirm who he is. Once again, as in act 1, scene 1, she is silent, and, once again, Lear tries to make sense of her muteness, to make "nothing" into something proper to him.

When they first see Lear staggering in with Cordelia, the three remaining characters form a chorus of responses that registers their shock and horror:

KENT   Is this the promised end?
EDGAR   Or image of that horror?
ALBANY   Fall, and cease.

(5.3.261–2)

Speaking for themselves, these characters speak also for the reader and audience, who have faced one cruel and unrelenting development after another. Scholars have heard in Edgar's modification of Kent's question an allusion to the Last Judgment, but one may also hear Edgar echoing words he himself had heard earlier in the play.[52] In act 1, scene 2, Edmund dupes Edgar into believing that their father was enraged against him, saying, "I have told you what I have seen and heard—but/faintly; *nothing like the image and horror of it*" (172–3, emphasis mine). Is the image of that horror now returning with the words? Is Edgar, seeing Lear, seeing himself imagining his father's rage—the horrible image of which threatened to annihilate his previous image of himself in the kingdom as his father's heir, and the threat of which he had to destroy? He has just vanquished this threat and reappeared to others in the kingdom precisely as the image of Gloucester's heir, an image that he has had in turn reflected back to him by others. Does seeing Lear now shatter that circuit of recognition and expose his fundamental difference from any given image that might settle the question of who he is? Does Edgar see belatedly now the blindness in his own seeing?

In the Folio, Edgar is given the last lines of the play to pose preliminarily the question of what it is to have seen *King Lear*. To see as Edgar has seen, the play shows, is to view oneself and others as members who have titles and parts proper to the kingdom as a closed and finite realm, and thus to succeed King Lear by perpetuating this framework of comprehending oneself and others. According to this logic, the generation that comes after would be merely the *next* instead of the *new*—thus denying the unscripted and unpredictable futurity that genuine newness implies. But the play interrupts the complicity of our viewing with Edgar to issue to the spectator the challenge of succeeding *King Lear* in a way that gestures toward the possibility of a future beyond the disaster it dramatizes. To succeed *King Lear* is to be addressed by the event of "nothing" the play performs—that keeps the kingdom one views from being stabilized as whole, and one's view from being whole or even a partial perspective on the whole.

I have tried, throughout this chapter, to pursue a sustained analysis of the ways the play allegorizes its own conditions of viewing. *King Lear* puts into complex operation the familiar idea of the *theatrum mundi*, derived from classical and early Christian sources and a guiding metaphor for the arts in the Renaissance and Baroque eras.[53] When the Globe Theater opened in London in 1599, it bore the motto, "Totus mundus agit histrionem." The most famous and explicit enunciation of this metaphor is, of course, by Jaques in *As You Like It*: "All the world's a stage/And all the men and women merely players."[54] In *King Lear*, Lear tells Gloucester, "When we are born we cry that we are come/To this great stage of fools" (4.6.178–9). In another vein but an inflection nonetheless of the concept of viewing oneself as being on view for others, Gloucester cries, "As flies to wanton boys are we to the gods,/They kill us for their sport" (4.1.38–9).

As Gloucester's lament indicates, God or the gods constitute the model spectator in the traditional understanding of the world as stage, with humans serving as actors. In the tradition of political theology, the king is the earthly representative of God, whose sovereignty reflects the sovereignty of God, in relation to which subjects are oriented as actors and constituted as spectators who see themselves and each other on view for God and king. Gloucester's lament expresses the idea that tragedy befalls when this system of reflective relationships goes awry, when the gods act like "wanton boys"—or "wanton boys" like gods.

Gloucester's reference to the gods stands out in a tragedy that features, for Shakespeare, an unusual lack of supernatural phenomena and scarce mention of divine forces. There are no ghosts or witches, and God or gods seem to be absent. *King Lear* shows the characters reckoning with this disappearance, and itself reckons with this disappearance by putting into question the traditional conception of the *theatrum mundi*.

The play exposes again and again cracks in the system of reflective relationships whereby characters appear to each other as actors and spectators, cracks that suggest the absence of a model spectator and a perspective on the whole. And it shows again and again the efforts of characters to deny this absence of mastery by themselves reconstituting sovereign perspectives on a kingdom stabilized again and again as a totality available to being viewed and, like an object, grasped and known. The play thereby also puts into question the traditional philosophical privileging of the intelligible over the sensible, dichotomously construed, which attends the traditional conception of the *theatrum mundi*. The tendency of characters to reconstitute perspectives on the kingdom as whole—what I call the cycle of tragic repetition—has for its paradigmatic figure Oedipus at the end of *Oedipus Tyrannos*, who reestablishes himself as master over the world as space of appearances by blinding himself after discovering the metaphorical blindness of his own lack of knowledge. *King Lear* shows the complicity of characters caught in this tragic cycle in unwittingly destroying their world.

King Lear, in my reading, is a tragedy that, paradoxically, opens a *way out* of the cycle of tragic repetition. It does so by asking us to bear witness to the event of Cordelia's "nothing." It shows us first how Cordelia's "nothing" exposes the limits of Lear's theater of sovereignty and then how the Fool sustains this legacy; in the second half it turns to exposing the limits of the theater of sovereignty Edgar resurrects in the wake of the debilitation of the play's fathers. In so doing, it enacts an exposure beyond the exposure whereby the spectator is constituted as sovereign and unitary in opposition to the world as spectacle, whereby she is situated outside the world as if the latter were a stage. The play *exposes*, then, not by maintaining a topological distribution of inside/outside, inclusion/exclusion, but by making perceptible to the spectator the "nothing" that structures her perceiving *among* others *in* the world as a space of appearances. This event of "nothing" cannot be converted to something with positive content and assimilated to a given program or agenda. It opens onto the future not as enveloped by the perspective of the present but as radically unknown and unconditioned. It addresses the spectator by calling upon her as an actor capable of freely performing an act beyond the act, for which there is no model or script. The world that emerges to view in this exposure beyond exposure is radically incomplete and always in the process of being created, always in excess of any kingdom or community conceived according to identifiable predicates of belonging. *King Lear* is a literary event that calls upon the spectator to participate in this *theatrum mundi*.

II.   *Wordsworth*

2. *Wordsworth on the Heath*

Tragedy, Autobiography, and the Revolutionary Spectator

What does Shakespearean tragedy have to do with Wordsworth's origination of a new and revolutionary way of writing poetry in the wake of the French Revolution? In what way might Wordsworth's poetic project be read in terms of an effort to succeed *King Lear*?

From the perspective of standard literary history, these questions will appear eccentric. Wordsworth is traditionally considered the primary Romantic descendant in a line of English poets that includes Chaucer, Spenser, and Milton and that harks back to Virgil as classical model.[1] Wordsworth himself supports this account, laying claim particularly to the legacy of Milton in references and allusions throughout his writings, most prominently in *The Prelude* and the Prospectus to *The Excursion*. In these latter works, Wordsworth explicitly announces his ambition to succeed Milton by updating visionary, prophetic epic for his own times, for the generations of readers who lived through and after the French Revolution, which was for him, as is well-known, far and away the paramount, defining event of his age.

These questions may appear odd also when one considers the vast, even antipodal, difference in style between Wordsworth and Shakespeare. In Keats's memorable formulation, Wordsworth is the poet of the "egotistical sublime," unmistakably the hero at the center of his own poems, who seems even with his characters to be speaking in propria persona. Shakespeare, on the other hand, is the impersonal dramatist par excellence, who was "everything and nothing," who could inhabit a variety of characters from Iago to Imogen without appearing in any way as the hero of his work.[2]

Yet, early in his career, before he inscribed himself into the legacy of Milton, Wordsworth composed in 1796–7 and revised by 1799 a tragedy in five acts that was obviously and extensively influenced by Shakespeare. *The Borderers* was Wordsworth's one and only play and, significantly, his first major effort alongside his long narrative poem *Salisbury Plain*. Situated beyond his juvenilia and at the threshold of his mature oeuvre, *The Borderers* is perhaps best described as a work of apprenticeship and has received critical attention principally for the light it can shed on Wordsworth's later trajectory. He wrote it at a time when his closest peers were writing plays: Coleridge was writing his own tragedy, *Osorio*, later called *Remorse*, for submission to Covent Garden after he had already collaborated with Southey on *The Fall of Robespierre*.[3] Wordsworth also submitted his completed play to one of the principal actors at Covent Garden for review but recalls it as having been "*judiciously* returned as not calculated for the stage," although he would have appreciated its acceptance given the state of his finances at the time.[4] The manuscript "lay nearly from that time till within the last two or three months unregarded among my papers," as Wordsworth writes in 1842, "without being mentioned even to my most intimate friends" ("1842 Note," 813). In more than one sense, then, *The Borderers* was a "closet drama." Forty-five years after completing the play, Wordsworth finally published it in 1842, changing the names of the characters and modifying passages but keeping the text otherwise substantially intact.

The Borderers is set in the thirteenth-century reign of Henry III and the Crusades in the border territory between England and Scotland disputed in the Baronial Wars. There are four main characters, named in the 1796–7 version Mortimer, Rivers, Herbert, and Matilda.[5] Mortimer is the leader of a band of border brigands who is manipulated by his associate Rivers into harming Herbert, the blind, old father of his childhood sweetheart, Matilda, whom Mortimer wishes to marry. Such, in nuce, is what takes place plotwise in this notoriously convoluted play that features numerous borrowings from *King Lear*, *Othello*, and *Macbeth*, with significant parts of the action taking place on the heath, where the play ultimately ends. The relationship between Herbert and Matilda shows significant resemblance to the relationship between Lear and Cordelia, with lines given to Herbert coming almost verbatim out of *Lear*. The character Rivers, as Wordsworth acknowledges in a prefatory essay to the earlier edition, is based on Iago. And the setting is reminiscent of the landscapes of both *Lear* and *Macbeth*. What brought Wordsworth, at this point in his career, to write this play? And what led him to base it so extensively on Shakespearean tragedy?

According to Wordsworth's own account, the French Revolution lay at the root of his initiative to write the play in the first place. At the end of the note appended to the play in 1842, Wordsworth recalls, "During my long residence in France, while the Revolution was rapidly advancing to its extreme of wickedness, I had frequent opportunities of being an eye-witness of this process, and it was while that knowledge was fresh upon my memory, that the Tragedy of 'The Borderers' was composed" (813). In 1843, he told his friend and the chief scribe of his old age, Isabella Fenwick, that the play was based on "what I had observed of transition in character & the reflections I had been led to make during the time I was a witness of the changes through which the French Revolution passed" (815). In these backward critical-autobiographical glances, Wordsworth regards his early play as an allegory of his experiences as witness of the French Revolution. Through *The Borderers*, then, Wordsworth can be seen responding to and reflecting on a course of events marked by such turning points as the storming of the Bastille and the executions of Louis XVI and Robespierre, as well as—on an autobiographical level—his own residence in France from 1791 to 1792 and continued involvement with revolutionary circles in England afterward.

Critics have responded to the invitation implicit in Wordsworth's remarks to interpret *The Borderers* as a combination of autobiographical and revolutionary allegory. As such, it has been read in several ways: as the poet's rejection of the attitude that had led him to expound the necessity of revolutionary violence in his 1793 "Letter to the Bishop of Llandaff"; as his renunciation of Godwinian theories of political justice that he had adopted after entering Godwin's circle in London in 1795; and as a coded confession in which Wordsworth revisits obliquely a misdeed he himself may have committed during his stay in France in 1791–2.[6] Wordsworth is supposed by many commentators to parade and review in *The Borderers* shades of partisan allegiance he tried on and then cast off in the years leading up to 1796–7.

The Borderers is indeed profoundly concerned with the relationship between autobiography and revolutionary democratic politics. But what makes this play for Wordsworth a remarkable and pathbreaking step in the direction of literary originality, I propose, is the way it puts the very relationship between autobiography and politics fundamentally into question. While many critics have interpreted the play as an *autobiography of politics*— that is, as a coded autobiography that looks back and sheds light on the poet's notoriously variable political positions and opinions—the play in fact goes further and interrogates the very *politics of autobiography*. What is the significance in democratic modernity of autobiography for politics, and politics for autobiography? In what terms would the autobiographical subject be a democratic political subject? I investigate in this chapter how Wordsworth raises these questions by rewriting Shakespearean tragedy after the French Revolution in *The Borderers*. I examine the political significance of autobiography for the characters within the play, studying how they relate to each other by telling stories about themselves. By examining what takes place between the characters *within* the play, I discuss how Wordsworth as playwright and poet learned from Shakespeare and attempts to succeed *King Lear* in his creation of a new and revolutionary poetics.

✦

First of all, what is autobiography? At the simplest level, prior to its classification as a genre, autobiography is the answer to the question, who are you? And how has this question engaged the literary tradition of tragedy? Roughly speaking, in ancient and early modern tragedy, the protagonist's answer to this question would typically be along the lines of: I am king, or I am a general or some kind of person of high birth or rank who has authority over others and commands their respect. The hero's identity is determined in advance by an established hierarchical system in which he or she occupies a central and elevated, if not *the* central and supreme, position. The question "who are you?" is not an active one for the hero at the outset of a drama, but rather becomes so only in the course of the play as a function of the hero's fall from the established, elevated position. "Who are you?" is not an active but a settled question for Oedipus, who thinks he knows who he is, but in the course of *Oedipus Tyrannos* finds out that he does not. Likewise, "who are you?" is not an active but a settled question for Lear, who even after abdicating has trouble releasing himself from the expectation that others should obey him whenever he commands, and that the world reflect back to him consistently his status as sovereign. "Who are you?" becomes a question for Hamlet when the answer established by right of birth and secured by the law of succession gets destabilized when his mother marries Claudius.

In contrast, "who are you?" has already actively preoccupied characters in *The Borderers* before the play even begins: Herbert has a readily available life story that he is not only fond himself of retelling but also has taught his daughter to repeat; Rivers too has a life story he is ready to tell Mortimer after he has made Mortimer into what would be for him the perfect auditor; and, at the end of the play, Mortimer asks his band of borderers to erect a monument on the heath on which his story would be inscribed for future readers. Not only are these characters concerned with telling stories about themselves for and by themselves, they use autobiography as the preeminent form of interpellating others.

When Wordsworth reminisces to Isabella Fenwick in 1843 about the process of writing the play, he remarks that, at the expense of refining plot and filling in details of character, "my care was almost exclusively given to the passions & the characters, & the position in which the persons in the Drama stood relatively to each other, that the reader (for I had then no thought of the Stage) might be moved & to a degree instructed by lights penetrating somewhat into the depths of our Nature" (814). Indeed, the reader is not provided with such details as the color of Matilda's eyes, Mortimer's build, or the timbre of Rivers's voice; but her attention is directed to how these characters relate to one another and are affected in their passions by participating in the world as a web of autobiographies.

How is it that autobiography acquires such importance in the dramatic world of *The Borderers*? Within the play, the autobiographical imperative emerges when one is dispossessed from one's identity as given within an established, traditional framework. Herbert begins telling his life story—and the story itself in fact begins—with the loss of his vision, his wife, and his son in a fire at Antioch and, upon his return to England from the Holy Land, his baronial holdings too. Returning home, he finds that he is no longer who or what he was when he left: a nobleman who embarked on a crusade with the clear mission of fighting the infidels. His usurpation from this previous identity is the condition for his autobiographical narrative. Rivers begins telling his life story, starting with his deception by his crewmates on their way to the Holy Land into mutinying against the ship's captain. This seduction into criminality forms the basis for his story of himself.

Significantly, both these autobiographies originate abroad or at sea, away from the sovereign domain of England, and they are repeated in the present of the play before the reader or the audience in the no-man's-land between England and Scotland. In these stories, Herbert and Rivers not only reestablish who they are for and by themselves, they also reestablish and legitimate their authority and power vis-à-vis others. Herbert uses his story to compel his daughter to obey him; Rivers uses his story to set himself up as an exemplary model for Mortimer to follow and to emulate.

In *The Borderers*, autobiographical storytelling emerges as a means of establishing authority. With this feature, Wordsworth departs from the tradition of ancient and early modern tragedy, and brings tragedy into the era of revolutionary modernity. In earlier tragedy, authority derives from the very framework of hierarchy. Instead of having to tell a story about himself to legitimate his authority, Lear simply gives orders and continues to do so even after he has abdicated the throne. Lear's authority derives from his supreme position in a hierarchy, in which the relation between the one who commands and the one who obeys is determined by the sheer fact of hierarchy itself. In *Oedipus Tyrannos*, Oedipus exercises authority likewise by virtue of being king of Thebes, a position he was qualified for by birth but which he thought he won by means of his intelligence in outwitting the Sphinx. Because authority is not grounded in a stable hierarchy of ruler and ruled, characters in *The Borderers* resort to autobiography as instrument of authority. This, I suggest, marks the play's contemporaneity with the French Revolution.

In keeping with the principle of universal humanity, the French Revolution introduced an egalitarian framework in place of a hierarchical one. In the transfer of sovereignty from the monarch to "the people"—the *demos* of democracy—every human being qua citizen of a democratic nation-state is supposed to be at once in relation to his fellows both sovereign and subject, ruler and ruled. Authority loses its basis in hierarchy, and the question of who somebody *is* is no longer simply determined beforehand according to rank, birth, or a predictable pattern of succession. Answering this question will entail, in the words of Rousseau at the beginning of his own exemplary autobiography, "a work which is without precedent" and "whose accomplishment will have no imitator," in which the autobiographical subject claims that "I am not made like any one I have been acquainted with, perhaps like no one in existence."[7] The task of answering this question is one of the central tasks of democratic modernity.

To elaborate on the political significance of autobiography, I turn briefly to the philosopher Hannah Arendt, who considers in *The Human Condition* how answering the question of who one is constitutes *the* quintessential political action.[8] Her book is dedicated to examining the *vita activa*, the life of action, classically the counterpart of the *vita contemplativa*, the life of the mind. The *vita activa*, insofar as it involves the activity of doing something, always takes place in a world among men, whereas the *vita contemplativa* involves withdrawal from the presence of others, although it too is fundamentally conditioned by the fact that the world is where human beings live together in the plural. Arendt divides the *vita activa* into three kinds of activities: labor, work, and action. Labor is necessary for biological survival. Work produces objects for use and exchange, which can be owned as property. In labor and work, human beings do not relate directly to one another but deal with the intermediary of matter and things. Only in action do human beings relate to one another directly and as equal yet unique human beings, each the same in such a way that each is un-exchangeable with any other.

Answering the question of who one is constitutes the quintessential political action through which every human being discloses her uniqueness and makes her distinct appearance in the human world. This disclosure repeats but surpasses the biological fact of natality, for being humanly alive is not merely to be alive in the way that plants and animals are. To be humanly alive entails a second birth beyond the physical, in which I insert myself as newcomer into a human world of speech and action that has already existed before me and that will survive after me. "This insertion," Arendt writes, "is not forced upon us by necessity, like labor, and it is not prompted by utility, like work."[9] It is an exercise of freedom. The principle of freedom comes into the world with every human being's disclosure of who she is through speech and action, which is a new beginning she makes in the world.

The manifestation of who someone is cannot take place in isolation but is necessarily an appearing to others in a world where one lives together with other men. The disclosure of singularity depends, paradoxically, on the fact of plurality—which Arendt takes as axiomatic in her project of rethinking politics against the philosophical tradition's tendency to think politics according to the abstraction of man in the singular. From the traditional perspective, a plurality of men would appear simply, according to an arithmetic logic, as a quantity of many countable units of man. For Arendt, man in the singular is unique but not unitary; man in the singular is already essentially plural and essentially non-unitary, fragmented. Arendt initiates, then, the pathbreaking and crucial intellectual agenda of thinking plurality in the singular, a difficult task involving a logic of paradox that she leaves as her intellectual legacy.

Answering the question of who one is, then, involves what might be called "autobiography-in-the plural," a life story with one hero at the center that does not, however, form a complete, discrete unit but is essentially exposed to an infinite plurality of other life stories, which precisely have the effect of keeping it from forming a discrete unit. Autobiography-in-the-plural is what, I claim, Wordsworth attempts to dramatize in his juxtaposition of autobiographies in *The Borderers*. Before returning to Wordsworth, however, I address two related points Arendt makes that will help explicate issues in the play.

First, she discusses the common risk of confusing the question of *who* somebody is with *what* somebody is. *What*ness has for its answer a description of attributes or qualities that one may have in similarity with others like himself or herself, wherein one is reduced to a type or "a 'character' in the old meaning of the word."[10] Romeo is young, wellborn, probably handsome, and occasionally eloquent. The *who*ness and specific difference of Romeo, however, escapes and exceeds such an enumeration of properties that makes him interchangeable with other wellborn, handsome, and eloquent young male "characters," in the old meaning of the word.

The question of *what* someone is takes as its object a substance-like entity that can be named and known, which possesses such and such properties that are in turn also like substances. Answering the question of *who* someone is entails, on the other hand, surpassing the tendency to think the realm of human affairs—of what takes place directly between men—in terms of an analogy with matter or things. If "what are you?" is a question in which the "you" is addressed as a substantive, "who are you?" addresses the "you" as an agent whose response to the question manifests itself not as an object but precisely through action.

Second, in describing this autobiographical agent, Arendt makes an important distinction between being the author of one's life story and being its actor: "Although everybody started his life by inserting himself into the human world through action and speech, nobody is the author or producer of his own life story. In other words, the stories, the results of action and speech, reveal an agent, but this agent is not an author or producer. Somebody began it and is its subject in the twofold sense of the word, namely, its actor and sufferer, but nobody is its author."[11] To be the author or producer of one's own life story involves relating to this story as if it were a fabricated and completed object, the answer to the question "what are you?" which can then be used as an instrument at one's disposal. It involves an implicit denial of the unpredictability of action, which sets into process in the world an outcome of which nobody can claim to be the author.

To relate to one's own life story as its author or producer would imply putting oneself in a position outside this story and abstracting it from the world of human relationships in which this story takes place, as if one could observe both one's own story and the world of human affairs from a completely external perspective (e.g., from beyond the grave or from the God-like perspective of the disinterested, sovereign spectator). To be part of the living world of human affairs means, however, that one is not the master of one's own life story but rather expropriated from this story in the process of enacting it. One is the actor of one's life story.

More precisely, in Arendt's formulation, one is actor-and-sufferer: active to the extent that one begins something new in the world but passive insofar as this beginning is never absolute but conditioned, the condition being the world itself. The world is, in this case, not the object of a unitary sovereign spectator but rather the immanent space of betweenness where human beings live together among one another. As actor, one lives among and is exposed to a plurality of other actors in relation to whom one is also spectator. One sees and hears others precisely *as* one who is also seen and heard by others. Insofar as participation in the active life entails on a fundamental level seeing and hearing others and being seen and heard by others, theater emerges among the arts as the political art par excellence that has the power to show us something about the way we live together, and how each relates to each in living together.

I return to *The Borderers* to investigate it as a political theater of autobiographies in which the characters relate to each other as actors, authors, and spectators, and are affected in their passions through the medium of their life stories. I focus my analysis on the quartet of main characters—Herbert, Matilda, Mortimer, and Rivers—and discuss, to begin with, how their interactions are structured by two life stories among them, those of Herbert and Rivers.

Before entering the maze of the play itself, however, I would like to consider again the question of the characters' Shakespearean antecedents, a question that pertains both to these characters' status as newcomers in relation to preceding literary characters and to Wordsworth's status as newcomer in finding and founding his poetic project. Herbert combines aspects of Lear and Gloucester, and Rivers, as Wordsworth acknowledges, is patterned on Iago. But these characters are not just by themselves of Shakespearean provenance, they are also part of pairings that likewise originate in Shakespeare. Rivers and Mortimer also recall, to a lesser extent, the fraternal pairing of Edmund and Edgar in *King Lear*. Herbert and Matilda recall Lear and Cordelia, Rivers and Mortimer Iago and Othello. It is significant that Matilda and Mortimer do not by themselves resemble Cordelia or Othello. Rather, if they are to be considered in a derivative light, it is not in relation to literary precursors but in relation to Herbert and Rivers as dominant characters. In their elliptical relationship to literary tradition, Matilda and

Mortimer represent the possibility of a genuinely new future that does not merely repeat the past, if only they could emerge from the control of Herbert and Rivers.

Why and how does Wordsworth bring together elements of *King Lear* and *Othello*? Like *King Lear*, *The Borderers* dramatizes a conflict between generations that is essentially related to a conflict within one generation. Rivers's manipulation and deception of Mortimer in the play constitutes both an interruption and subversion of Herbert as representative of patriarchal authority, and an attempt to substitute his autobiography in place of Herbert's as the master narrative for the characters concerned. But unlike the bastard Edmund in *King Lear*, whose ambitions remain articulated by a patriarchal hierarchy that he wishes to climb, Rivers's ambition is neither to usurp Mortimer's position as leader of the borderers nor to assume the patriarchal authority operative through Herbert. His aim is not merely to revolt or rebel within a stable hierarchical system wherein one hierarchical regime is replaced by another, but to undermine the system altogether and to introduce a new model of authority. In such nihilistic passion, he resembles Iago more than any other character and, beyond Iago, displays what might be called "revolutionary fundamentalism." Wordsworth combines elements of *Lear* and *Othello* to create a drama of intergenerational conflict that goes beyond a logic of revolt wherein hierarchy remains intact. He combines elements of the two plays to comment on the specificity of his own revolutionary times—a move of the newcomer that implicitly sheds light on and departs from Shakespeare as predecessor in the annals of literary succession. In the writing of the play, Wordsworth enacts a drama that resonates with what takes place in the play itself.

I begin my analysis of *The Borderers* with the figure of Herbert, who occupies the position of predecessor in the play. This predecessor is also a patriarch. For a long time, readers of the play regarded Herbert as a benign and helpless old man, the entirely innocent victim of Rivers's machinations and Mortimer's weakness. In his several essays on the play, however, Reeve Parker has compellingly established that while Herbert may be victim, he is far from benign.[12] Rather, Herbert is the author of an autobiographical master narrative that keeps his daughter, Matilda, in a subordinate position and thus prevents her from being the hero of her own story. In relation to Herbert's autobiography, according to Parker's reading, Matilda resembles a ventriloquist's dummy. I agree with this interpretation but wish to inflect it with the notion of the child as prosthetic device; Matilda functions as the dummy that makes Herbert whole. To read Herbert skeptically is thus to exceed the position of Matilda as credulous listener who receives her father's life story unquestioningly.

Wordsworth presents this story as one coherent narrative right at the outset of the play in the first scene of the first act, fittingly in the context of a dialogue between father and child. The pair is taking a rest while journeying together to receive a bequest from Matilda's patroness. Reference is made to a previous conversation about Mortimer's courtship of Matilda, to which Herbert poses strenuous objection. Matilda has already acceded to Herbert's wishes but begins now to tell again the story she has been taught since childhood to repeat like a catechism:

> But think not, think not, father, I forget
> The history of that lamentable night
> When, Antioch blazing to her topmost towers,
> You rushed into the murderous flames, returned
> Blind as the grave, but, as you oft have told me,
> You clasped your infant daughter to your heart.
>
> (1.1.144–9)

Parker notes that the narrative itself figuratively repeats this physical clasp, for Herbert's "tale has the effect of binding [Matilda] to him by rousing in her an obsessive, ruling gratitude."[13] The dialogue resembles more of a monologue since Matilda's part in it has been scripted in advance by her father. Herbert continues on seamlessly from where Matilda leaves off, as if their two voices were one:

> Thy mother too—scarce had I gained the door—
> I caught her voice, she threw herself upon me,
> I felt thy infant brother in her arms,
> She saw my blasted face—a tide of soldiers
> That instant rushed between us, and I heard
> Her last death-shriek, distinct among a thousand.
>
> (1.1.150–5)

And Matilda begs him, "Nay, father, stop not, let me hear it all:/'Twill do me good" (1.1.156–7), showing the effectiveness of the narrative as an instrument that enthralls her by eliciting the sense of filial duty it served to instill in the first place. At her prompting, Herbert remarks before returning to the story: "Dear daughter, dearest love—/For my old age it doth remain with thee / To make it what thou wilt" (1.1.157–9).

His interjection makes it appear here as if it were entirely her choice, and none of his, to assume the task of his care. Then he continues retelling the story before ending this segment of their conversation by reiterating his objection to Mortimer:

> Thou hast been told
> That when, on our return from Palestine,
> I found that my domains had been usurped,
> I took thee in my arms, and we began
> Our wanderings together. Providence
> At length conducted us to Rossland. There
> Our melancholy story moved a stranger
> To take thee to her home; and for myself,
> Soon after, the good abbot of Saint Cuthbert's
> Supplied my helplessness with food and raiment,
> And, as thou knowest, gave me that little cottage
> Where now I dwell.—For many years I bore
> Thy absence, till old age and fresh infirmities,
> Now six months gone, exacted thy return.
> I did not think that during that long absence
> My child, forgetful of the name of Herbert,
> Had given her love to a base freebooter
> Who here, upon the borders of the Tweed,
> Doth prey alike on two distracted countries,
> Traitor to both.

> (1.1.159–78)

Matilda had started to recite the story in the first place to demonstrate again her loyalty to her father and her submission to his judgment—after she had already written a letter of rejection to Mortimer. Herbert's story serves as an instrument for compelling obedience from Matilda, who, despite her own desires, accedes to Herbert's will. The conversation had begun with Herbert's hearing and interpretation of Matilda's silence: "You are silent./That is a silence which I know" (1.1.103–4). He claims omniscience even over her silence, and she submits by crying:

> Wherefore thus reproach me?
> When I behold the ruins of that face,
> Those eye-balls dark—dark beyond hope of light,

And think that they were blasted for my sake,
The name of Mortimer is blown away;
Father, I would not change this proud delight
For the best hopes of love.

$$(\text{1.1.105–11})$$

Herbert's blindness serves as a mechanism to evoke her sense of filial self-sacrifice, which she calls here "this proud delight"—a mixture of obligation and pleasure that anticipates what Nietzsche will find characteristic of "slave morality."

Now that the story has been retold in detail, let us take a closer look. Herbert's story answers the question of who he is, as he became at Antioch, where one might say he underwent a fall and rebirth, where the story of a new self began. Previous to the watershed events of that "lamentable night," he was a baron who had gone with his family to the Holy Land on a crusade. On that night, he acquires by means of his story a glorious new identity as a self-sacrificing rescuer—a hero who lost his vision while saving his daughter, who was parted from his wife and son in the process, and who would subsequently discover upon returning to England that he had been usurped of his possessions.

At the origin of this narrative was an event of blinding. As an empirical event, this blinding is to be distinguished from its thematization within a narrative that Herbert uses to give significance to his life. In and through the story, blindness becomes the condition for his new identity as self-sacrificing savior, a function of the act of saving itself. But Herbert *suffered* the blinding; that is to say, he was not the controlling agent but entirely passive in the event of being physically wounded. His story, however, denies this passivity and links this suffering with a saving, an act of which he can claim verily to have been the author. The link that transforms his passive suffering into an active saving is encapsulated in the preposition "for," as Matilda makes evident when she says, "When I behold the ruins of that face,/Those eye-balls dark . . ./And think that they were blasted *for* my sake" (emphasis mine). Herbert was not just blinded, then; he was blinded for Matilda. The wound as site of the body's vulnerability becomes instead the sign of his new victim's authority.

The narrative compensates for his losses and performs the work of restoration in two ways. First, it assimilates the events of that watershed night into a pattern of salvation consistent with Herbert's identity as a crusader who had gone with his family to Palestine to save it from the infidels. Herbert is a fallen baron whose story affirms qualities of valor and self-sacrifice, qualities of the crusading savior who has sworn loyalty to God and His earthly representative, the King, and whose mandate thus continues to define him within a vertical patriarchal system despite the fact of usurpation. (Indeed, Henry III will invisibly and belatedly affect Herbert's fate from a distance later in the play when, in a *basileus ex machina*, he restores Herbert's hereditary land and title to him.) Second, the story implicates and defines his daughter, Matilda, in such a way that she must compensate for the loss of his eyes by serving as his eyes, and thus performing for him the prosthetic function of being a lesser part of a preconceived totality that would make him whole again.

By establishing him as a savior, his autobiography also inspires in his daughter, as Parker has argued, the reciprocal passion to save and protect him.[14] Through her, his story reached Mortimer, who recounts how, as a child: "It was my joy to sit and hear Matilda / Repeat her father's terrible adventures / Till all the band of play-mates wept together, / And that was the beginning of my love" (1.1.65–8). And that perhaps was also the beginning of his own impulse, along with his grown-up band of borderers, to patrol the countryside saving and protecting innocent civilians. Herbert's story stands at the head of a chain of listeners who model themselves after him as rescuers. He is not only the author of his own life story but, through this story, the author as maker of others whose deviation from the script he does not condone. When Matilda cries of Mortimer, "O could you hear his voice!" Herbert does not wish to hear Mortimer's voice. Nor can he hear Matilda's voice when she at this point deviates from his master narrative.

Strikingly, the possibility of Matilda's own story emerges precisely when she speaks—in her own voice—of hearing the voice of another man, even if that other man's voice may be, like hers, almost completely dominated by her father's voice. Herbert objects to Mortimer because Mortimer is an outlaw whose allegiances are unclear, "a base freebooter / Who here, upon the borders of the Tweed, / Doth prey alike on two distracted countries, / Traitor to both," in comparison to whom he sustains the principle of undivided, unambiguous loyalty. As crusading savior, Herbert had distinguished clearly between friend and enemy, and he continues afterward to uphold the law of the King, according to which Mortimer would be automatically defined as criminal or outlaw.

It is the patriarchal authority Herbert represents that Rivers seeks to subvert, supposedly on behalf of Mortimer. Rivers tries to undo the grip of Herbert's master narrative on Mortimer by means of an intricate ruse that exploits the weaknesses of Herbert's story, and the inferable fact that there are no other witnesses—Matilda having been an infant at Antioch—who can confirm the story's veracity. A mysterious stranger whose life Mortimer has recently saved, Rivers has been dispatched just before the beginning of the play as Mortimer's emissary to ask Herbert for Matilda's hand in marriage.

But Rivers is an unreliable emissary who uses his position to dispute and foment suspicion over Herbert's story and thus to turn Mortimer against Herbert. He manipulates Mortimer into thinking that Herbert is not Matilda's birth father and that Herbert plans even to sell Matilda into sexual bondage to the disreputable Lord Clifford. He pays a beggar woman to claim that she is the real mother of Matilda and that she had handed Matilda over to Herbert in infancy. Through such complex orchestration, Rivers substitutes in Mortimer's mind an alternative story in place of Herbert's own story. Mortimer, convinced he must save Matilda, is persuaded that he must kill Herbert. Unable to do so outright, however, Mortimer abandons Herbert on the heath at night, forgetting to give him his scrip of food and thus effectively leaving him to die of cold and hunger.

While Wordsworth presents Herbert's life story to the reader or audience right in the first scene of the play, he does so by framing the dialogue between Herbert and Matilda with a preceding conversation between Rivers and Mortimer. Rivers reports to Mortimer Herbert's objections—

> For that another in his child's affection
> Should hold a place, as if 't were robbery,
> He seemed to quarrel with the very thought.
> Besides, I know not what strange prejudice
> Seems rooted in his heart: this band of ours,
> Which you've collected for the noblest ends,
> Here on the savage confines of the Tweed
> To guard the innocent, he calls us outlaws
>
> (1.1.28–35)

—and he begins to cast aspersions on Herbert's story: "The tale of this his quondam Barony / Is cunningly devised" (1.1.52–3). When they see Herbert and Matilda approach, they hide behind a thicket and overhear the dialogue that ensues. Thus Rivers relates to Herbert's story in terms of a "framing" in both senses of the word: by overhearing it alongside Mortimer and also by exploiting its weaknesses to spin, in relation to selected fragments, an alternative story. If Mortimer, like Matilda, is a credulous, unquestioning listener vis-à-vis Herbert's story, Rivers is the model of the attentive and suspicious listener, a variety of critical reader who contests the authority of the master narrative and operates on its periphery to unravel it. Subverting Herbert's central and authoritative story of the father as self-sacrificing rescuer, Rivers exchanges it for a variant version of the father as fraud and pimp.

While establishing this variant version, Rivers engages in activities much like that of a playwright or director. He enlists the Beggar woman like a paid actress to speak lines he has scripted for her. He rewrites Herbert's script and, loosening its power over Mortimer, manipulates Mortimer like a puppet. If Herbert has occupied in the past the position of the central playwright who speaks ventriloquistically through Matilda and Mortimer, Rivers emerges within the present action of the play as a counter-playwright who undermines and denaturalizes Herbert's patriarchal authority. Following his subversion of Herbert's story, the staging of which he considers complete once Mortimer has abandoned Herbert on the heath, Rivers makes a surprising transition from playwright to autobiographer. The mysterious stranger emerges from the wings, as it were, to tell his life story to Mortimer, starting with the admission, "I shall be able / To throw some light on this part of my history / You are unacquainted with—I am a murderer" (5.2.2–4).

Rivers does not only tell his own story but, through its telling, reveals to Mortimer that he has just implicated Mortimer in a situation in which he himself had been implicated in the past. On their way to the Holy Land, Rivers was duped by his crewmates into thinking that their ship's captain was conspiring against his honor; and he was thus convinced that he needed to defend that honor by abandoning the captain on a barren island. The rest of the crew then admitted that the captain was innocent and that Rivers had been the unwitting instrument of their mutinous plot. Rivers claims to have arrived afterward at an epiphany whereby he was liberated from conventional morality. From his new perspective, the "crime" in which he was implicated was no crime; and he would be an autonomous, self-legislating individual who heeds the authority of reason alone and not the law of others who together constitute society. He sets himself up as a liberator who communicates this message to Mortimer after staging a spectacle in which Mortimer has likewise abandoned a man to his death—a man who, Rivers now reveals, is innocent of the conspiracy Rivers had concocted.

Let us consider Rivers's story more closely now, first by comparison with Herbert's story. If Herbert's story begins not with earlier events in his life but with the watershed night at Antioch, Rivers's story likewise does not dwell on what he was prior to leaving England but with the shipboard events that culminate on the barren island. Previous to those events, Rivers was a youth who, as he tells Mortimer, "was the pleasure of all hearts—the darling/Of every tongue—as you are now" (4.2.5–7), favored even by the captain's daughter to watch over her father. The story that begins at sea is thus the story of a new self, a rebirth that is predicated on the fall from a position taken as given. If at the beginning of Herbert's story was an event of blinding of which he was not the author but a passive sufferer, at the beginning of Rivers's story was an action of which he was likewise not the author but—as unwitting agent—in a significant sense passive. Rivers served as a means to an end in a way he could neither predict nor control; he was a puppet manipulated by his crewmates. For him to assert to Mortimer, "I am a murderer," is to elide an ambiguity inherent in his situation, a passivity at the very heart of his action.

Rivers speaks the play's most famous and oft-quoted lines, which address precisely the theme of action:[15]

> Action is transitory, a step, a blow—
> The motion of a muscle—this way or that—
> 'Tis done—and in the after vacancy
> We wonder at ourselves like men betray'd,
> Suffering is permanent, obscure and dark,
> And has the nature of infinity.
>
> (3.5.60–5)

He speaks these lines to Mortimer in an earlier attempt, before the telling of his personal story, to win Mortimer over to his post-epiphanic perspective. These pseudo-tutelary comments allude to Rivers's own involvement in an action of which he was not the author but a puppet, and the syntax he uses here to speak of action mimics the jerky, uncoordinated movements of a marionette. The comments are spoken from the perspective of one who has wondered at himself in the "after vacancy" of action, who is responding to his experience of the non-sovereign nature of action and who claims now to be able to transmit the lesson of his recovery from this experience.[16]

In the story he tells Mortimer, Rivers recounts how, after the events at sea, he retreated to a convent in Palestine for three nights and began there a process of restoration that culminated in a visionary revelation on the summit of Mount Lebanon in Syria, where he "perceived/What mighty objects do impress their forms/To build up this our intellectual being" (4.2.133–5). Setting himself apart from the other crusaders, Rivers recalls:

> When from these forms I turned to contemplate
> The opinions and the uses of the world,
> I seemed a being who had passed alone
> Beyond the visible barriers of the world
> And travelled into things to come.

(4.2.141–5)

And he concludes:

> That we are praised by men because they see in us
> The image of themselves; that a great mind
> Outruns its age and is pursued with obliquy
> Because its movements are not understood.
> I felt that to be truly the world's friend,
> We must become the object of its hate.

(4.2.152–7)

In the "after vacancy" of action, Rivers claims to have attained a form of visionary transcendence whereby, as Wordsworth explains in his prefatory essay on the character, he "pictur[es] possible forms of society where his crimes would no longer be crimes, and he would enjoy that estimation to which from his intellectual attainments he deems himself entitled" (64–5). Rivers absolves himself from any taint of criminality by setting himself outside the laws of others, construing himself—like Robespierre—as a "great mind" subject to reason alone. Having thus liberated himself, he preaches to Mortimer a message of liberation:

> To day you have thrown off a tyranny
> That lives but by the torpid acquiescence
> Of our emasculated souls, the tyranny
> Of moralists and saints and lawgivers.
> You have obeyed the only law that wisdom
> Can ever recognize: the immediate law
> Flashed from the light of circumstances
> Upon an independent intellect.
> Henceforth new prospects ought to open on you,
> Your faculties should grow with the occasion.

(3.5.26–35)

Joined "by a chain of adamant," they would thus constitute the founding members of a new, post-patriarchal fraternity: "Henceforth we are fellow-labourers—to enlarge / The intellectual empire of mankind. / 'Tis slavery—

all is slavery, we receive / Laws, and we ask not whence those laws have come" (4.2.187–91). Rivers tells Mortimer his life story to create solidarity between them after he has manipulated Mortimer like a puppet into becoming his double, "a shadow of myself / Made by myself" (5.2.32–3). This history is the paradigmatic story of the prophetic liberator, the model after which the empire of "fellow-labourers" is to be made.

Rivers's story answers the question of "who am I?" by taking the "I" outside the living world of human affairs in which the "I" would figure as an actor among other actors, a spectator among other spectators, one who sees and hears while being seen and heard by others. He retreats behind the scenes, as it were, to observe the world seeing but unseen. In relation to this completely external position, the world appears to him as an object that is the collection of false perspectives—*doxa*, or the opinions and uses of the world. The world appears then as an object that can be totally overthrown or remade. In relation to his own life story, Rivers tries to establish mastery as author. In relation to others, Rivers assumes the role of a playwright who manipulates others toward the end of substituting his own script; and then, beginning with Mortimer, he introduces his new, post-patriarchal master narrative.

If Herbert's story serves a restorative function by symbolically compensating for his usurpation, nostalgically evoking his belonging to a system from which he has been exiled, Rivers's story serves a restorative function by seeking to destroy this system altogether. Rivers is a proponent of revolutionary fundamentalism—in other words, of terrorism. What does his story restore? What is the nature of the loss from which Rivers attempts, through creating his life story, to recover?

As he tells Mortimer, he is "a murderer." Before he became a murderer (which may be an overstatement) he was "the pleasure of all hearts—the darling / Of every tongue—as you are now." He was deceived, betrayed, manipulated into participating in an action in which he was a puppet. When the ship reached land, "The tale was spread abroad—my power shrunk from me, / My plans of heroism, my lofty hopes, / All vanished—I could not support the change" (4.2.75–7). The crisis happened when Rivers finds that the world no longer sees him as the darling, when his *image* has been compromised: that is, the image of himself that he wants the world to see. He cannot *show* himself before the world as he had planned, cannot control his appearing as an *appearance*. In this conception, the world that Rivers wants to see him may be compared to an audience waiting for him as leading actor to appear on stage as the favorite of the theater of holy war.

Interestingly, for Rivers, although the crew had deceived him, he does not selectively target them as his enemies but makes the entire world, or the world as entirety, the object of his hatred. The crew he in fact *blesses* for making him what he is: a man who has transcended the opinions and uses of the world and looks upon the world as an object. Interestingly, Rivers does not express after the fact either antipathy or regret vis-à-vis the captain. He recalls the island where they left him as follows:

> 'Twas a spot—
> Methinks I see it now—how in the sun
> Its stony surface glittered like a shield:
> It swarmed with shapes of life scarce visible;
> And in that miserable place we left him—
> A giant body mid a world of beings
> Not one of which could give him any aid,
> Living or dead.

$$(4.2.37–44)$$

The spot returns to Rivers as memory and image of a place. On this spot the captain would die as a man who is literally not seen and heard by others. "'Twas an island/But by permission of the winds and waves;/I know not how he perish'd," Rivers tells a stunned Mortimer (4.2.57–9).

What is the significance of the island? Why did the crew plot to leave the captain there? The island is a place outside the borders and the claims of sovereign, juridical-political domains, a *non-place* in juridical-political terms that the ship stopped by en route from England to the Holy Land. In this non-place outside the law the crew leaves the captain to die without directly murdering him—that is, without technically committing homicide.[17] They leave him to die an unwitnessed death, in the company of "swarming shapes of life," "a world of beings," none of them human.

Rivers calls this island "a world of beings." For him, this world is separate from, outside of, the world in which he had hoped to appear on stage as darling actor. The Holy Land, on the other hand, is a continuous part of the world as his stage of appearance. The island is an instance of the exception that founds the political topology of sovereign domains. What takes place on the island shatters for Rivers the image he hopes to project on the "real" stage. The event on the island is related to this "real" stage, however, by leaving a stain or spot on the way Rivers wants to appear there.

As a result, Rivers becomes disenchanted with this "real stage," and with the terms of the drama unfolding there, "despis[ing] alike Mahommedan and Christian," as one of Mortimer's borderers recalls at the beginning of the 1842 version. He thus claims a perspective beyond the "real stage," going beyond the world as a collection of "false" opinions and uses to a position of truth. In claiming this position, which he arrives at in solitude on the peak of Mount Lebanon, Rivers can be said to create a strange symmetry between himself and the captain—both are outcasts from the world of opinions and uses. He overcomes the spot that taints the way he is seen by transforming it into a position where he is not seen but all-seeing.

As "spot," the island is not just a geographical site. It is internalized as a site in Rivers's personal topography, his memory, a site that links him to the abandoned captain, a site that haunts his present seeing but whose haunting he tries to overcome and stabilize. He tells Mortimer his story from his newfound spot, aiming to win him over to this privileged new location from which to view the world. His story, however, has a different effect on his listener than what he had intended.

Mortimer's life story emerges out of its implication with Rivers's story. When Rivers starts telling Mortimer about the island where the captain was abandoned, Mortimer interjects a description to supplement Rivers's account:

> A man by men deserted,
> Not buried in the sand—not dead nor dying,
> But standing, walking—stretching forth his arms:
> In all things like yourselves, but in the agony
> With which he called for mercy—and even so,
> He was forsaken.

$$(4.2.44-9)$$

At this point, Mortimer does not yet know that Herbert is innocent. But the image he conjures up while listening to Rivers evokes Herbert's probable predicament in the present on the site of the heath, a landscape that in its inhospitality resembles the topography of the island.

The heath is the scene of a repetition, a site uncannily haunted by another scene. Both heath and island are non-places outside of sovereign jurisdiction, exceptional border territories that form the outside whereby the juridical-political domain—and the juridical-political domain as space of appearances—gets constituted. If the island was internalized by Rivers as a spot in memory, the heath becomes for Mortimer a haunted site when he hears Rivers telling his own story, as he realizes how he has been implicated and manipulated by Rivers. The heath becomes for Mortimer a haunted site where he cannot see or hear what happens to Herbert, how Herbert dies. The unwitnessed death of Herbert forms an immemorial blind spot in Mortimer's consciousness.

Mortimer tries to search on the heath for Herbert and runs into a peasant, Robert, who recounts how he had come across Herbert earlier but had abandoned him again for fear of getting into trouble. Robert had been wrongfully imprisoned before and will not risk helping another man. Herbert's unwitnessed death haunts Mortimer. To die a human death, for Mortimer, is to die in the company of other human beings—an idea he expresses when he recalls:

> the first riddle that employed my fancy,
> To hunt out reasons why the wisest thing
> That the earth owns should never chuse to die
> But some one must be near to count his groans.—
> The wounded deer retires to solitude—
> And dies in solitude—all things but man,
> All die in solitude—an awful lesson.

(5.3.31–7)

While other animals die apart from their kind, Mortimer ponders, the human being typically performs and suffers the last act of his life in the presence of others. Upon other human beings the story of his life depends, for it is they who, perceiving what the agent as actor and sufferer cannot perceive, bear witness to and assume responsibility for the agent's life as that which always exceeds his own, proper authority. In his responsibility for the other's death qua responsibility for the life story of the other, Mortimer has failed. This failure manifests itself as a lacuna in his own story.[18]

What will Mortimer's story be? What constitutes Mortimer's answer to the question, who are you? Will he exit from the author structure of Herbert and Rivers's autobiographies? *The Borderers* presents a succession of stories: Herbert's, Rivers's, and finally Mortimer's. I have suggested that Wordsworth is trying to open up the possibility of autobiography-in-the-plural, a way of enacting one's life story that is non-sovereign but exposed to human plurality. To do so is to succeed *King Lear*—to succeed the play and to succeed where the play's characters fail. What happens on the heath as it returns as topos from *King Lear* in *The Borderers*?

If Herbert's and Rivers's stories both begin with a fall from their previous identities, so does Mortimer's own story. Mortimer's story may be said to begin again on the heath, as Herbert's did at Antioch and Rivers's on the desert island. His story begins as a function of the conflict between the other two stories, each of which casts him in a different role. Herbert and Rivers are not only the authors of their own life stories but, vis-à-vis others, sovereign playwrights who attempt to make others conform to their own scripts. Forgetting the scrip(t) of one, Mortimer unwittingly acts in the play of another. Wordsworth as playwright shows how Mortimer is caught between these two scripts. How will Mortimer's destiny take shape? What kind of new birth takes place on the heath?

The heath becomes the site of a new storytelling. Mortimer leaves Rivers's script behind to look for Herbert. Learning that Herbert has died, he confesses to Matilda, "I am the murderer of thy father" (5.3.99). This confession resonates with Rivers's assertion that he is a murderer in likewise eliding the ambiguity in the situation, the passivity inherent in—rather than opposed to—action. But this scene of storytelling is different from the other two in that it involves more than two interlocutors: it is not a scene of private tutelage in which autobiography is used instrumentally. Rather, the act of storytelling takes place in the context of trial or judgment. Mortimer and Matilda are surrounded by Robert and the Beggar woman, whose testimonies modify Mortimer's initial claim. Mortimer produces as evidence a letter that he and Herbert both signed, addressed to Matilda and drafted when he thought that Herbert was a fraud:

> Be not surprized if you hear that some signal judgment has befallen the man
> who calls himself your father—he is now with me, as his signature will
> shew—suspend your judgment till you see me—Herbert Mortimer
>
> (5.3.126–130)

The Beggar woman admits to taking a bribe from Rivers to mislead Mortimer. Revising his initial claim, then, Mortimer tells Matilda: "I led him to the middle of this heath. / I left him without food and so he died" (5.3.169–70). Matilda faints.

Mortimer's voice emerges at the end of the play first in this scene of judgment in which he acts, like Oedipus, as both prosecutor and defendant in his own trial. The beloved Matilda is his addressee in this case, the first recipient of his story. But Mortimer does not stop there. The audience within the play will not be his final court. He gives his men, who have killed Rivers in the meantime, this order:

Raise on this lonely Heath a monument
That may record my story for warning—
SEVERAL OF THE BAND (eagerly)   Captain!
MORTIMER

No prayers, no tears, but hear my doom in silence!
I will go forth a wanderer on the earth,
A shadowy thing, and as I wander on
No human ear shall ever hear my voice,
No human dwelling ever give me food
Or sleep or rest, and all the uncertain way
Shall be as darkness to me, as a waste
Unnamed by man! and I will wander on
Living by mere intensity of thought,
A thing by pain and thought compelled to live,
Yet loathing life, till heaven in mercy strike me
With blank forgetfulness—that I may die.

(5.3.262–75)

The task of telling Mortimer's story falls on the borderers then: the borderers within the play, and the audience or reader of the play. Mortimer's story
remains to be told. Its telling will emerge as the function of a reading. In
the meantime, Mortimer will assume the unwitnessed fate of Herbert and
constitute the wandering excess that keeps his story from being completely
known. As wandering excess, Mortimer's fate will constitute the blind spot
of the audience or reader's imagination.

Wordsworth gives Mortimer lines from *King Lear* at the end of the play.
Looking for Herbert, Mortimer asks Robert, "Have you seen/In any corner
of the savage heath/A feeble, helpless miserable wretch,/A poor, forsaken,
famished, blind old man?" (5.2.1–4) He quotes here Lear addressing the elements and referring to himself as "poor, infirm, weak, and despis'd old
man" (3.2.20). Mortimer cries to Robert about Herbert's dead body:
"Howl, howl, poor dog! Thou'lt never find him more;/Draggled with
storm and wet, howl, howl amain,/But not in my ears—I was not the death
of thee" (5.3.203–5). He echoes here Lear's cry as he carries Cordelia's dead
body in the final scene of the tragedy:

Howl, howl, howl, howl! O, you are men of stones!
Had I your tongues and eyes, I'd use them so
That heaven's vault should crack: she's gone for ever.

I know when one is dead and when one lives;
She's dead as earth. (*He lays her down.*)
          Lend me a looking glass.

                                                 (5.3.255–9)

Lear dies vainly trying to ascertain the life of the one he would make the preferred witness to his own death, whose life would serve as looking glass that confirms his authority over his own story. In having Mortimer echo Lear, Wordsworth makes reverberate a hollowness in Mortimer's own story that is not finally eradicated through the interpellation of the listener as dummy, puppet, or looking-glass double.

At the end of *The Borderers*, at the very border of the play itself, the heath emerges as the site of a new kind of storytelling. On this site, Mortimer's story will be told by a community of reader-listeners that must assume the responsibility of storytelling in his absence. Mortimer disowns authority over this story but commits himself to haunting it like a ghost. In the context of the play, Mortimer thus occasions a break with the patterns established by Herbert and Rivers. One tells the story of himself as wounded and wronged savior, the other as visionary liberator. In doing so, both try to overcome past events in which their status as agents were compromised, ambiguously suspended between activity and passivity. They try to establish authority over the passivity *inherent in* their actions by separating activity and passivity, dichotomizing being an actor and being a sufferer. They tell stories that firmly establish themselves as authors of their own lives, and address these stories to listeners whose lives they would script and manipulate. As a listener who has been caught between these stories, Mortimer refuses to continue this circuit of interpellation. He refuses to make the heath the privileged point of departure for a life story, as Herbert and Rivers had done with Antioch and the desert island, through which he restores mastery over himself and others.

Wordsworth attempts through Mortimer thus to exit a tragic theater of repetition. The break Mortimer occasions with Herbert and Rivers is a break with the pattern also of the paternal figures of Lear and Gloucester and the fraternal figures of Edmund and Edgar in *King Lear*. Wordsworth writes a tragedy to examine and go beyond the cycle of tragic repetition wherein the aggrieved seek redress for their injuries by unwittingly sustaining the very logic whereby they received injury in the first place. In writing

The Borderers, his first major work and only drama, then, Wordsworth undertakes implicitly a reading of the history of tragedy. He inscribes himself into this literary tradition so as to ex-scribe himself as poet-cum-historical-actor from the tragic cycle. Writing in 1796–7, Wordsworth undertakes in *The Borderers* at the same time a reading of history as tragic repetition, allegorizing his experience as actor and spectator in the theater of the French Revolution.

It is in the passage through tragedy that Wordsworth moves beyond the espousal of revolutionary violence in the "Letter to the Bishop of Llandaff" and the subscription to Godwin's theory of political justice—and toward a revolutionary, new mode of literary address to the reader qua democratic actor and spectator. Writing as "a man speaking to men," this most autobiographical of poets will address the reader not as an author in possession of his own life story but an actor who depends on the reader to bear witness to and assume responsibility for his story, as he himself witnesses and assumes responsibility for the life stories of others.

The heath figures as the site of this new mode of address. Wordsworth succeeds *King Lear* in inheriting and transforming this topos. Recalling the heath in *Lear* and the desert island in Rivers's autobiography, the heath in *The Borderers* is a site of exposure, a barren, inhospitable place that, in juridical-political terms, is a *non-place* between the sovereign jurisdictions of England and Scotland. For Lear and Edgar, the heath is a site of exile and exposure; but, converting the heath into an external vantage point from which to view the kingdom as finite whole and others qua members of this whole, they precisely avoid exposure *to* each other. Rivers likewise makes the desert island, the site of his betrayal, into a place from which he can contemplate the "opinions and uses of the world" as if he were not of the world but outside it. Rivers fails in his attempt to make the heath such a site for Mortimer, fails to make this addressee of his story a "fellow-labourer" who would embrace exposure outside the political realm as the condition of freedom. Instead, at the end of the play, the heath becomes the site of an "exposure beyond exposure"—beyond, that is, the exposure whereby kingdoms and individuals constitute their sovereignty by casting out and enforcing a strict divide between inside and outside. It becomes the site of an uncanny undecidability that unsettles the supposed integrity and consistency of borders and the communities of membership they enclose.

The heath is internalized as topos in Mortimer's consciousness, marking precisely what keeps his consciousness from being whole.[19] As the site where Herbert dies an unwitnessed death, the heath marks for Mortimer his failure to bear witness to and assume responsibility for another, a failure that renders his own story incomplete and improper, exposed to the unpredictable responsiveness and responsibility of others. Mortimer will not tell his own story but leaves this task to his borderers, who will inscribe his story on a monument while he wanders silent on the heath, haunting both site and story like a ghost. Reading Mortimer's story—an allegory for reading *The Borderers*—entails the encounter with this haunting as necessary part of the story. Wordsworth's originality in inheriting the topos of the heath consists of transforming it from a site of exposure outside the community into the basis of a new *locus communis* whereby community itself emerges in the readers' radical exposure to the life stories of others.

3. *Poetry against Indifference*

Responding to "The Discharged Soldier"

About suffering they were never wrong,
The Old Masters; how well they understood
Its human position; how it takes place
While someone else is eating or opening a window or just walking
dully along. . . .

W. H. Auden, "Musée des Beaux Arts"

La poésie ne s'impose plus, elle s'expose.

Paul Celan

A group of so-called encounter poems have become over the last twenty to thirty years the focal points of critical debates over the political implications of Wordsworth's poetry. These poems have in common the narrator's encounter with vagrants, the rural poor, or ethnically marginal groups—the old Cumberland beggar, the discharged soldier, gypsies, the leech-gatherer—and have been related to similar episodes in *The Prelude*, such as the encounters with the blind beggar and the hunger-bitten girl. Critical positions taken with respect to these poems range from defenses of how Wordsworth displays and promotes sympathetic solidarity with the poor and how he challenges middle-class readers to confront the possibility of their own impoverishment, to condemnations of how his poems display instead sympathetic solidarity with the bourgeois reader at the expense of an aestheticized poor.[1] In and through these polemics, Wordsworth seems to have emerged effectively as preeminent poetic symptom and test case for the inner contradictions of modern liberal political thought.

As a generic term, the "encounter poem" may have a source or at least significant antecedent in Frederick Garber's 1971 *Wordsworth and the Poetry of Encounter*, which examines Wordsworth's poems as self-conscious epistemological exercises in which the poet reflects on the operations of his own mind in its encounter with various objects.[2] In Garber's study, the objects of encounter were not specified as the homeless or poor per se, but as *whatever* objects of the poet's intentional consciousness, such as nuts, daffodils, or the voice of the solitary reaper. This ecumenism faded as the phenomenological approach to Romanticism, and above all Wordsworth, was accused by historicist and materialist readers of participating too sympathetically and uncritically in the poet's own "idealizing" tendencies, for colluding in the alleged Romantic escape from, or denial of, the realm of history and politics. With the shift in critical temper, the "encounter poem" has come by and large to be defined according to the category of socioeconomic class and thus to designate encounters with specifically the homeless and the poor.

In this chapter I focus on one particular "encounter poem," perhaps the earliest one that Wordsworth wrote that would fit the criteria of the "encounter poem," however defined. Wordsworth wrote "The Discharged Soldier" between January and March of 1798 at a crucial moment in his career: around the time of finishing "The Ruined Cottage" and conceiving of *The Recluse* project, and shortly before writing many of the poems that would go into *Lyrical Ballads*. He did not publish "The Discharged Soldier" as an independent lyric. Significantly, however, he did plan for it—along with "A Night-piece," "The Old Cumberland Beggar," and "The Ruined Cottage"—to form one of the introductions to *The Recluse*, the encyclopedic poem on "Man, Nature, and Human Life" that would include *The Prelude* and *The Excursion* but that was never completed.[3] Each of these introductory poems, all written in 1798 around the time of the conception of *The Recluse*, somehow looks forward to or actually became part of another, longer work. "The Old Cumberland Beggar" became part of *Lyrical Ballads*, "The Ruined Cottage" part of *The Excursion,* and "The Discharged Soldier"—anticipating Wordsworth's autobiographical turn—part of *The Prelude*, concluding book 4, on "summer vacation."

These four introductory poems feature certain affinities. "A Nightpiece" and "The Discharged Soldier" have been paired together as companion poems insofar as both feature a solitary walker enjoying a moment of peaceful restoration in nature.[4] On the other hand, "The Discharged Soldier" has also been paired as a companion poem with "The Old Cumberland Beggar," since both feature a vagrant personage who is isolated from and seemingly indifferent to the society of other human beings. Crucially, "The Discharged Soldier" is split between these two poems. "The Discharged Soldier" and "The Old Cumberland Beggar" share, moreover, a striking intertextual affinity. The soldier's proverbial saying, possibly an adaptation of Lamentations 1:12—"My trust is in the God of Heaven,/And in the eye of him that passes me" (162–3)—returns in the last lines of "The Old Cumberland Beggar"—"As in the eye of Nature he has lived,/So in the eye of Nature let him die" (188–9).[5]

But they are in other respects very different poems. Rhetorically, "The Old Cumberland Beggar" is a polemical intervention addressed explicitly to "Statesmen" in order to persuade them, for the sake of a typical local community, not to support workhouses and to let beggars be as they are. "The Discharged Soldier" makes no such statement on behalf of either the soldier or the community; in fact, it provides no explicit statement about how it is to be read. It does not style itself as an intervention nor attach itself positively to any side of an existing political debate. It simply narrates the remembrance of an event that took place ten years prior (in 1788) that was of formative importance for the poet's mind.[6]

In book 12 of the 1805 *Prelude*, Wordsworth recounts how, while he was growing up, the public road was for him a school out of school where he learned from meetings with vagrants: "the lonely roads/Were schools to me in which I daily read/With most delight the passions of mankind" (163–5).[7] He recalls how:

> in those wanderings deeply did I feel
> How we mislead each other, above all
> How books mislead us—looking for their fame
> To judgements of the wealthy few, who see
> By artificial lights—how they debase
> The many for the pleasure of those few.

> (205–10)

"The Discharged Soldier" rehearses one such lesson in the autobiography of the poet who would in 1800 articulate the democratic ambition of transforming English poetry by basing it not on the diction of a select tribe of poets but on the language spoken by a multitude of speakers—indeed, on the language of "real men." Besides narrating an episode from the past, "The Discharged Soldier" is one such event in the language of man speaking to men. What the poem crucially shows is that this language is not simply known or available in advance, as if it were a demotic idiom waiting for the poet to collect and transcribe. What "The Discharged Soldier" shows, rather, is precisely the precariousness and contingency of a democratic poetic language, and the necessity of its continual and interminable rediscovery.

☙

The title of this chapter alludes to a term Wordsworth uses several times in the poem to describe aspects of his conversation with the soldier. "A short while," he recalls, "I held discourse on things *indifferent*/ And casual matter" (90–1, emphasis mine). In listening to the soldier tell his story, Wordsworth discerns a manner of speaking that was "neither slow nor eager, but unmoved,/ . . . a quiet uncomplaining voice,/ A stately air of mild *indifference*" (95–7, emphasis mine); and later again, he speaks of hearing "a strange half-absence and a tone/ Of weakness and *indifference*, as of one/ Remembering the importance of his theme,/ But feeling it no longer" (141–4, emphasis mine). Closely synonymous here with "apathy," "indifference" bespeaks an impasse of feeling, of pathos, in the soldier's relationship to his own speech, as well as an impasse that blocks communication between the two men. The soldier uses language but without feeling; the two men use language to communicate, but they do so without mutual feeling or sympathy. "Indifference" marks, from Wordsworth's narratorial perspective, a crisis in the language of man speaking to man, a crisis defined precisely by the absence of perceptible mutual feeling.

Wordsworth responds doubly to this indifference: as passerby in the actual meeting, then again as poet who narrates the memory in a poem. The actual meeting took place in the summer of 1788 on the public road three miles from Hawkshead, where the eighteen-year-old Wordsworth had returned from Cambridge on vacation. Wordsworth was out taking a walk at night when he came across a stranger. He observed the stranger for some time, noticing his faded uniform, before hailing him and talking with him. After a while, Wordsworth proposed that they walk back toward the cottage of a laborer he knew so that the soldier could find food and lodging for the night. They walked and reached the cottage. Before parting, Wordsworth asked the soldier not to linger any more in the public ways but to seek help from others. As mentioned above, the soldier replied with an expression, which possibly adapts a scriptural quotation—"My trust is in the God of Heaven/ And in the eye of him that passes me"—that seemed to Wordsworth to convey the "same ghastly mildness" he had shown before.[8] He then thanked Wordsworth, Wordsworth returned the "blessing," and so they parted.

The indifference of the soldier's speech was just one sign for Wordsworth of the soldier's lack of mutual feeling or interest in being part of the world with other human beings. Before talking with the soldier, Wordsworth had already noted visible signs of his indifference to the company of others, summarizing his observations thus: "he appeared/Forlorn and desolate, a man cut off/From all his kind, and more than half detached/From his own nature" (57–9). In the way he looked and the way he spoke, the soldier seemed to Wordsworth a spectral presence who belonged more to the realm of the dead than the living. Accordingly, Wordsworth alludes to Milton's description of Death in book 2 of *Paradise Lost* in details of the soldier's "ghastly" appearance; and to Dante's journey through hell with Virgil when he writes, "Together on we pass'd,/In silence, through the shades gloomy and dark" (146–7).[9] While the soldier was biologically alive, as plants and animals are, he seemed to Wordsworth only ambiguously alive insofar as being humanly alive entails living among other human beings, however that *living among* is construed. "Thus the language of the Romans," according to the philosopher Hannah Arendt, "perhaps the most political people we have known, used the words 'to live' and 'to be among men' (*inter homines esse*) or 'to die' and 'to cease to be among men' (*inter homines esse desinere*) as synonyms."[10] For the discharged soldier to appear to Wordsworth only ambiguously alive is tantamount to his appearing only ambiguously alive *among men*.

As passerby, Wordsworth had attempted to respond to this indifference by bringing the obviously weary and emaciated soldier to the laborer's cottage where he could find food and shelter, mediating between the soldier and the world of other human beings, even offering to reimburse the laborer for his expenses. But he did not stop there. His parting exchange with the soldier bespeaks a desire to prolong the effects of the mediation by making it a precedent for the soldier rather than a punctual, one-time occurrence. He thus asked the soldier "henceforth" not to linger in the public ways but to seek relief or alms, as he has presumably shown him how to do by intervening. The soldier's first reply seems to show no change, but rather a continued fatalistic indifference that renders uncertain the future of the mediation. What Wordsworth wanted from the soldier can be succinctly expressed in the phrase "reviving interest," which he claimed to hear when the soldier thanked him "in a voice that seem'd/To speak with a reviving interest,/Till then unfelt" (166–8). As passerby, Wordsworth had acted to help the soldier by guiding him to the laborer's cottage. But he had hoped also to revive in the soldier feelings of interest in being among others, to generate an effect of sympathy. One sign of such interest would be if the soldier, no longer indifferent, showed some kind of sympathetic response. In the parting exchange, Wordsworth seems to have received mixed signals.

Recounting this actual meeting ten years later, "The Discharged Soldier" narrates, on one level, the story of a frustrated mediation. But the poem does more, of course, than just constatively report the story of what happened. In writing the poem, Wordsworth responds again to the soldier's indifference and performs anew the work of mediation. This new work of poetic mediation, I propose, allegorizes on a radical level what it is to mediate, to move *between*. The poem once again tries to revive interest, but it does so by reviving *inter-est* itself as a question, opening up as essentially unknown what it is to *live among* men.

Strikingly, the poem begins not with the encounter but with Wordsworth taking a walk alone at night on the public road. Indeed, the first thirty-five lines could stand by themselves and constitute an independent poem that would serve as the perfect companion for "A Night-piece." They commemorate an experience in which Wordsworth finds restoration for his exhausted mind by bringing it into contact with the natural landscape, and celebrate the benefits of walking alone. When Wordsworth recounts after this opening that "a sudden turning of the road/Presented to my view an uncouth shape" (37–8), the turn is likewise sudden for the reader. From the perspective of its beginning, the poem can be said to tell the story of a solitary walk interrupted by the encounter with another solitary. Through this construction of the poem as if it consisted of two parts, I suggest, "The Discharged Soldier" opens up for examination the relationship between being alone and being with others, two modes of human existence usually polarized as opposites.

Wordsworth begins by declaring a love for walking on the public way at night because the road assumes at this time an aspect of solitude so at odds with its daytime character that the contrast makes it seem even more private than unmarked paths. What does solitude let him do that he could not do otherwise? In short, it lets him imagine. Solitude lets his mind conjure up "absent things" in response to the natural objects he perceives. He recounts one specific walk as follows:

> I slowly mounted up a steep ascent
> Where the road's watry surface to the ridge

Of that sharp rising glittered in the moon
And seemed before my eyes another stream
Stealing with silent lapse to join the brook
That murmured in the valley.

(5–10)

He creates first a visual analogy between the road and a stream, and then a parallel across the senses of sight and hearing when he likens the stream-like road to the murmuring brook. His mind brings associations to the sensory data his eyes and ears receive, and thereby creates new abstractions. In this way, he revitalizes "an exhausted mind worn out by toil" (16) and derives "a restoration like the calm of sleep/But sweeter far" (23–4). In this process, the public road seems for Wordsworth—to leap ahead to a future art—the screening room for his own nocturnal road movie:

What beauteous pictures now
Rose in harmonious imagery—they rose
As from some distant region of my soul
And came along like dreams, yet such as left
Obscurely mingled with their passing forms
A consciousness of animal delight,
A self-possession felt in every pause
And every gentle movement of my frame.

(28–35)

It is uncanny how these verses anticipate and resonate with cinema as an allegory of the mind's own operations.

Why is solitude the condition for imagination? Let us take a brief explanatory detour from Wordsworth's public road to Hannah Arendt's account of mental activities in *The Life of the Mind*.[11] As the title indicates, this book is dedicated to what is traditionally called the *vita contemplativa*, and it complements her earlier work, *The Human Condition*, dedicated to the *vita activa*. The *vita activa* has to do with the realm of action as a world of appearances, in which human beings live among each other and are available to each other as objects of the senses. From the perspective of the world of appearances, the *vita contemplativa*, the life of the mind, is in hiding or seclusion, for thinking involves withdrawal from the world of appearances: the activity of the thinker is manifest only negatively in the world of appearances in the form of what is called "absentmindedness." We are alone when we think because we have withdrawn from active involvement in the world of appearances, from the world of common sense shared in common with other men. In thinking, we challenge and exceed common sense, which, without the dynamic excess of thought, would leave us complacent, unchanging creatures of habit and routine.

Wordsworth cherishes his solitary walk as a retreat from the world of common-sense reality in which his "exhausted mind" was "worn out by toil." On this walk he does not appear to other human beings, and no others appear to him: "Above, before, behind,/Around me, all was peace and solitude:/I looked not round, nor did the solitude/Speak to my eye, but it was heard and felt" (24–7). In this retreat, he enjoys restoration and a "self-possession" that he could not enjoy while actively involved in the world of appearances. He is able to create new things that exceed common-sense, shared reality.

According to Arendt's analysis, the relationship between the life of the mind and the life of action has been conceived of by the philosophical tradition in dichotomous and hierarchical terms. In the Platonic-Cartesian tradition, the *vita activa*, the realm of action, has always been considered from the perspective of the *vita contemplativa*, with the latter always being granted a hierarchically superior position. The philosophical tradition is by and large characterized by the tendency to privilege the contemplative thinking of the whole, in which thinking takes one *outside* the world of appearances so that the world can be contemplated as spectacle. But, for Arendt, thinking's withdrawal from the world of appearances does not entail putting it in a privileged position: one does not leave the world of appearances and active involvement in it to a privileged position in order to contemplate the world as whole. Arendt's project of rethinking the relationship between the life of the mind and the life of action is a critique of the classical conception of thinking that secures the privilege of thought and constitutes the stability of its discourse by completing, in relation to thought, the world of appearances as a totality.

Where does Wordsworth stand in relation to this tradition? Is the public road another avatar of Plato's cave? My short answer is no—at least not in "The Discharged Soldier." This poem, I argue, enacts a non-dichotomous and non-hierarchical relationship between the life of the mind and the active life, between being alone and being among others. I return now to the public road, to the bend where Wordsworth's solitary walk is interrupted by the sudden appearance of the soldier.

The appearance of the soldier comes as a surprise. It interrupts Words-worth's erstwhile process of creating abstractions in response to natural sense objects. The phenomenon appears first to him as "an uncouth shape." Wordsworth does not immediately appear to the stranger, but delays this appearance by studying the soldier first from the shade of "a thick haw-thorn" where he "could mark him well,/Myself unseen" (40–41). At a cer-tain point, he approaches the soldier and "hails" him, beginning a conversation. Then, at a certain point in their exchange, he proposes to the soldier that they walk back to the cottage of a laborer of his acquaintance.

At least a couple of readers of the poem have echoed Wordsworth's own scruples about delaying his appearance to the soldier. The poet refers to hav-ing to subdue his "heart's specious cowardice" in order to leave "the shady nook where I had stood" to finally hail "the Stranger" (84–6). Alan Bewell comments: "Few, to my knowledge, have remarked on just how odd this scene is, with the poet timorously peering from behind a bush. The empha-sis upon his fearful vantage point, his 'prolonged . . . watch' (84), and the successive transformations that take place in the 'uncouth shape' first pre-sented to his view, recall the specular staging of the 'primitive encounter.' Not only do we see what the poet sees, but we also see him actively and fearfully constructing this image."[12] Undoubtedly, the poet's description of the soldier's physical appearance reflects elements of his own anxiety. Con-fronted with the stranger, Wordsworth describes him by inflating his height and alluding to the figure of Death in *Paradise Lost*. "Long time," he remarks, "I scanned him with a mingled sense/Of fear and sorrow" (67–8). But to judge Wordsworth here "cowardly" or indulging in "a minor act of ethical bad faith" would be to identify inherently with Wordsworth's own vantage point and thus to repeat vis-à-vis Wordsworth the narrator's own stance vis-à-vis the soldier.[13] To do so would be to miss the way the poem displaces and decenters the narrator's vantage point and registers a difference *within* that perspective.

I mentioned above two turning points in Wordsworth's meeting with the soldier: the moment when he approaches and hails the soldier, and the moment when he proposes they walk to the laborer's cottage. In both cases, what prompts these actions are sounds. In the first case, it is the sound of the mastiff's howl that serves as a cue for Wordsworth to act by appearing to the soldier. In the second case, it is the sound of a word, I suggest, that prompts Wordsworth to act and guide the soldier to the laborer's cottage for the night.

In the first instance, Wordsworth, still hidden from view, recalls register-
ing the presence of a village near the road, "whose silent doors / Were visible
among the scattered trees" (73–4). He remembers hearing the soldier murmuring, and then he remembers at this point:

> all the while
> The chained mastiff in his wooden house
> Was vexed, and from among the village trees
> Howled never ceasing. Not without reproach
> Had I prolonged my watch, and now confirmed,
> And my heart's specious cowardice subdued,
> I left the shady nook where I had stood
> And hailed the Stranger.
>
> (79–86)

In the second case, Wordsworth recounts in indirect discourse the personal
history the soldier tells in reply to Wordsworth's request, a standard-issue
soldier's tale that he tells "unmoved, / And with a quiet uncomplaining
voice, / A stately air of mild indifference" (95–7), namely:

> that he had been
> A Soldier, to the tropic isles had gone,
> Whence he had landed now some ten days past,
> That on his landing he had been dismiss'd,
> And with the little strength he yet had left
> Was travelling to regain his native home.
>
> (98–103)

"At this," Wordsworth recalls,

> I turned and through the trees look'd down
> Into the village—all were gone to rest,
> Nor smoke nor any taper light appear'd,
> But every silent window to the moon
> Shone with a yellow glitter. "No one there,"
> Said I, "is waking; we must measure back
> The way which we have come: behind yon wood
> A labourer dwells. . . .
>
> (104–11)

The deictic "this" in line 104, I propose, refers to the word "home" he
hears the soldier say. If the mastiff's bark prompts Wordsworth to appear to

the soldier, the sound of the word "home" cues Wordsworth associatively to think of the village and then the laborer's cottage as places where the soldier might, on his way home, travel in the world among men.

As passerby, Wordsworth had responded to the soldier's seeming indifference to being among men by guiding him to shelter for the night. It is uncertain, at the end of this mediation, if the soldier would "henceforth" go about his journey home in the manner Wordsworth would prefer him to—by asking for relief and alms along the way. The fate of the soldier remains as unknown as the fate of the intervention. That it is the word "home" that serves as Wordsworth's cue to intervene suggests that what is profoundly at stake and in question in the poem is how the world can be a home to both Wordsworth and the soldier. The poem gives us Wordsworth's vantage point, shows us his narrator's associations with the word "home"; and both *Prelude* versions add to the original ending verses on how the narrator himself, after parting with the soldier, sought "with quiet heart my distant home." "Home" is the signifier in the poem of destiny and destination. What the poem shows, beyond Wordsworth's vantage point, though, is the uncanniness—*die Unheimlichkeit*—inherent in the very assumption that there be *one* home for many.

I return now to the mastiff's howl, the sound that prompts Wordsworth to emerge out of the shadows and appear to the soldier. In the verses quoted above, Wordsworth first reports hearing the mastiff's howl from the direction of the village, then writes, "Not without reproach / Had I prolonged my watch" (82–3). Wordsworth hears the howl as a sign of reproach, a sign that he ought to "subdue" "[his] heart's specious cowardice" and finally hail the stranger. Appearing to another entails for Wordsworth, then, mastering his fear: appearing to another is here equivalent to appearing as one who has mastery over himself, who has, as we would say today, "gotten a hold of himself." Appearing to the soldier implies for Wordsworth appearing as a sovereign individual who can be responsible and reliable for the other. And appearing as such an individual is motivated by the feeling of guilt, associated with the community of men from which the mastiff's bark issues. To appear out of solitude to another, then, is to appear as a member of a community of men related to one another by ties of guilt and obligation—the contractual economy of debtors and creditors Nietzsche analyzes in the second essay of *On the Genealogy of Morals*.[14]

Significantly, the very same mastiff's howl returns in the poem. On their way back to the laborer's cottage, Wordsworth asked the soldier why he "tarried" on the public road instead of "demand[ing] rest / At inn or cottage" (126–7). In his reply, which Wordsworth renders in direct discourse, the soldier refers to the mastiff's howl:

> "My weakness made me loth to move, in truth
> I felt myself at ease, and much relieved,
> But that the village mastiff fretted me,
> And every second moment rang a peal
> Felt at my very heart—I do not know
> What ail'd him, but it seemed as if the dog
> Were howling to the murmur of the stream."
>
> (128–34)

This howl is the same howl—or an iteration in the same series—that Wordsworth writes of hearing earlier. The howl was heard by both men while they were on the public road, one hiding behind the hawthorn, the other leaning against the milestone unaware of being watched by the first. It is a sound object both men heard but that we learn at this point each has heard *differently*.

If Wordsworth heard the sound as a sign of reproach, how did the soldier hear the same sound? In his remarks above, he surmises the dog's howls indicated pain. Further, he creates an acoustic parallel between the rhythm of the dog's barking and the rhythm of the murmuring stream, giving evidence here of a solitary mental activity that had been phenomenally unavailable to the observer, manifest perhaps only in the enigmatic murmuring Wordsworth had heard earlier. But what I find most striking here about the soldier's remarks is that they are spoken not with *indifference* but with *feeling*: "every second moment [the mastiff] rang a peal, / Felt at my very heart" (131–2). The soldier uses language here with a feeling absent from the rest of his speech; he speaks with "reviving interest."

At the end of the poem, just before they part, Wordsworth claims to hear the soldier thank him in "a voice that seem'd / To speak with a reviving interest / Till then unfelt." Why then does he not make note of this earlier, unambiguous sign of interest and feeling from the soldier? Could it be that he simply did not hear it?

Obviously, the mastiff's howl is a sound that both men heard but did not hear in the same way. But the poem does not just juxtapose two different ways of hearing that are in communicative dialogue with each other—like a conversation in the green room. What the poem shows, rather, is a more fundamental and prior difference in ways of hearing that I explain with brief reference to the philosopher Jacques Rancière's concept of "disagreement," in French *la mésentente*.

At the beginning of the *Politics*, Aristotle defines man as political animal that has speech, distinguishing speech (*logos*) from voice (*phonos*), which is possessed by other animals. In this classic definition, voice is capable of communicating only pleasure and pain, while with speech human beings can express ideas about good and evil, justice and injustice, and deliberate the affairs they hold in common. To be a member of a community entails having speech. But what, Rancière asks, does it mean to have speech? What counts as having speech rather than merely making "noise" to express pleasure or pain? Politics, according to Rancière, takes place not because that question is settled but precisely when that question is raised, again and again—when a dispute arises over what it means to be perceived as having speech and thus to have a stake in the common. At stake also in such a dispute is the definition of the common itself, which is not a stable whole that consists of the sum of its parts but is rather essentially contingent and incomplete. This dispute is what Rancière terms "disagreement" or *mésentente*. [15]

What the poem of "The Discharged Soldier" shows is not just a difference in ways of hearing between two partners in communicative dialogue with each other but also a more fundamental difference or disagreement over what it means to speak and to be heard as a member of a community, as one who lives among men and speaks of interests held in common. It dramatizes an encounter between two incommensurable perspectives that nevertheless have to do with each other. And, astonishingly, it does so by preserving the incommensurability within it as an uncanny echo rather than by assimilating it to one perspective or the other. Let us examine the speech situation more closely.

The soldier speaks of discovering a parallel between the howl and the stream, and he speaks of hearing the mastiff's howl in a way that was "felt at his very heart." In this speech, he reveals a sensitivity to the voice of another animal and the pain it might indicate, but he marks himself apart from the animal by using language to express analogy and to communicate this analogy to another interlocutor. In this analogy he reveals something unique about himself that is specific to his experience, that makes him distinctive from other human beings. And he speaks here of and with feeling, a feeling absent, according to the narrator, from the rest of his speech. What does he speak of that the narrator notes is accompanied by a tone of "indifference"?

First, he tells his personal history in reply to Wordsworth's request, namely:

> that he had been
> A soldier, to the tropic isles had gone,
> Whence he had landed now some ten days past,
> That on his landing he had been dismiss'd,
> And with the little strength he yet had left
> Was travelling to regain his native home.
>
> (98–103)

And, later again, he speaks with "a strange half-absence, and a tone / Of weakness and indifference, as of one / Remembering the importance of his theme / But feeling it no longer." This time it is in reply to the narrator's questions "of what he had endured / From war, and battle, and the pestilence" (136–7). It is when he speaks *as* and of having been a soldier, then, that he speaks with indifference. The story he tells is a generic soldier's tale that could have been told by any one of the soldiers returning from the tropics. It is *une histoire reçue* in which he is represented as a passive object of logistical transport but from which a vital half is missing, a vital half in which he appears as an agent of speech and action.

How is it that the narrator does not perceive this sign of feeling but looks for it later, when the soldier thanks him? Precisely because, I propose, he looks for it elsewhere. The feeling of the other is not where I expect it to be and I myself want to feel it. Sympathy does not take place within a structure of sameness or symmetry but of radical asymmetry. To be sympathetic, then, involves exposure to the incommensurability of the pathos of the other. Contrary to what the narrator of "The Old Cumberland Beggar" asserts, we do *not* have all of us one human heart. Rather, what "The Discharged Soldier" shows is that the oneness of such a heart is a fantasy that denies the plurality and alterity of human *hearts*.

The narrator looks for a sign of "reviving interest / Till then unfelt" in the convention of thanking that serves as counterpart to the convention of hailing by which he had sought to interpellate the stranger. He returns the soldier's thanks by blessing "the poor unhappy man" (171), closing their encounter with a structure of exchange that bespeaks participation in an implicitly contractual economy. By asking the soldier "henceforth" not to linger in the public ways but to ask for relief or alms at inn or cottage, he was hoping to obtain a promise or guarantee from the soldier, as if the soldier were a reliable partner in a contract. Instead of such a promise, he gets an enigmatic reply: "My trust is in the God of Heaven / And in the eye of him that passes me."

Beyond the perspective of the narrator, the poem shows the inadequacy of his conception of community and what it is to live among other human beings. As passerby and as narrator, Wordsworth operated with an implicit understanding of the human being as one who lives among others as a sovereign individual capable of being contractually responsible and accountable to others. And this is how, emerging guiltily out of behind the hawthorn, he appears to the soldier and attempts to mediate for him. By telling the story of a frustrated mediation, however, the poem performs a new mediation that sheds light on the inadequacy of the prior mediation, that shows the community inherent in the contractual conception as essentially inadequate and incomplete, *not*-whole.

The poem enacts a new logic of mediation based on the radical asymmetry of human perspectives rather than on symmetry and commensurability. It opens up the possibility of politics by dramatizing as an unsettled and inconclusive question what it means to be perceived as having speech and thus to have a stake in the common. In doing so, it calls for a responsiveness prior to responsibility and displaces and decenters the perspective of the narrator, which frames for the reader the entire encounter. But it does not just go beyond the perspective of the narrator as if establishing for the reader as sovereign individual a supra-perspective that is outside of those of the narrator and the soldier, so that the reader can in turn contemplate the poem as a whole. Rather, the poem reveals the inadequacy and incompleteness of the narrator's perspective precisely *through* the narrator's perspective. And that is precisely wherein, I claim, the *poetic* greatness and originality of Wordsworth lies.

The mastiff's howl, as I have said, returns in the poem. The entire poem narrates in the autobiographical mode a memory of Wordsworth's. And both times the mastiff's howl, as textual phenomenon, appears to the reader as part of this memory. The first time it appears from within the perspective of the narrator. The second time it appears likewise within the perspective of the narrator, but in the remembered words spoken by the soldier. That is to say, the second time it appears as an undigested, foreign kernel within the narrator's framing perspective, a discontinuity within his conscious understanding that persists nonetheless in his memory like a wound. The mastiff's howl returns in the text as an uncanny echo of its first appearance from within the perspective of the narrator, an echo that marks precisely what is unassimilable to the narrator's perspective but is nevertheless implicated within it—the unknownness of the other. In the return of the howl, the narration falls silent.[16] The howl that persists within memory as a hole in understanding is simultaneously what keeps the self from completing itself as known and thus from collapsing into identity with the thinking ego: it keeps Wordsworth from being the sovereign master of his own story. Through this effect of echo, the poem makes reverberate a silence to the reader, who likewise cannot herself look upon the story of the poet from a completely external perspective, but must relate to his story precisely through his falling silent.

In telling the soldier's speech about the mastiff's howl, the narrator's situation may be compared to that of the boy of Winander when the owls stop responding to his mimic hootings, when the sensory world stops reflecting back what his mind projects. The silence in "The Discharged Soldier" is not a literal silence, of course, but the effect of the narrator's not hearing in the soldier's words what his mind projects. This silence exposes the narrator to what lies *outside* his own perspective—not to the outside as a world beyond the world but to the outside as a plurality of perspectives opening onto worlds incommensurable with his own. At this moment, Wordsworth is, without his knowing it, "as if admonished from another world" (1805 *Prelude* 7.623). Like the leech-gatherer, the discharged soldier was to him "like a man from some far region sent." This other world and this other far region may have something to do perhaps with that "distant region of my soul" from which "beauteous pictures / Rose in harmonious imagery" for the solitary walker at the beginning of "The Discharged Soldier," whose solitude was perhaps not so absolute.

In conclusion, I turn to the modification of the soldier's saying, "My trust is in the God of Heaven, / And in the eye of him that passes me," at the end of "The Old Cumberland Beggar": "As in the eye of Nature he has lived, / So in the eye of Nature let him die." For what purpose does Wordsworth borrow the soldier's authority, itself an instance of borrowed authority, to conclude a poem that supposedly serves as companion piece for "The Discharged Soldier"? Might "The Old Cumberland Beggar" be read as an alternative response to the soldier's indifference, yet another attempt at mediation?

If "The Discharged Soldier" opens up the possibility of a responsiveness prior to responsibility, "The Old Cumberland Beggar" offers the model of an unresponsiveness that stabilizes the realm of responsibility. By situating the beggar outside the community for which he serves as record of charity, the narrator can secure the wholeness and unity of the community, affirming that "we have all of us one human heart." On the other hand, he can stabilize nature as a world beyond the world, that serves as the *outside* to the community. Through this move, he creates a perspective from which to contemplate the community as the picture of a juridical-political entity under the jurisdiction of statesmen with whom he may deliberate. Further, he secures in Nature a locus of freedom—from "industry" and the claims of living among human beings—where the solitary human being can leave the world of appearances and be seen only by the eye of a benevolent Nature. The relationship between being alone and being with others is dichotomized again here. The beggar emerges as the figure of "bare life" in relation to which, as Giorgio Agamben has argued, sovereign power defines itself, with Wordsworth writing another chapter in a tradition of political theology that has persisted well beyond the revolutionary transfer of sovereignty from monarchs to nation-states.[17]

"The Discharged Soldier" and "The Old Cumberland Beggar" exemplify abiding tendencies in Wordsworth's work, and the tension between them persists elsewhere. In retelling the memory of meeting the soldier at the end of book 4 of *The Prelude*, Wordsworth omits in both 1805 and 1850 versions the return in the soldier's words of the mastiff's howl. The passage remains a haunted and haunting remembrance, the narrator remains perplexed by the soldier's unaccountable indifference, but access is lost to another human world through the perspective of another human being. It is when Wordsworth least knows it that his poetry has most to offer the future of politics.

III.   *Agee and Evans*

4. From the Division of Labor to the Discovery of the Common

James Agee and Walker Evans's
Let Us Now Praise Famous Men

What kind of a work is *Let Us Now Praise Famous Men*? The question continues to baffle interpreters almost seventy years after the 1941 publication of this unpredictable, idiosyncratic, and extravagant work that fits so uneasily under its prevailing classification as documentary journalism. It isn't even clear whether the work is complete, as one of its authors, James Agee, indicates in his preface—"the present volume is merely portent and fragment, experiment, dissonant prologue," one of a trilogy of works, the two others of which were never finished. Perhaps the question should be more properly phrased to ask, what kind of a work in progress is *Let Us Now Praise Famous Men*?

The question is, on the face of it, a generic one. Setting aside the auxiliary problem of what to call Agee's text—which moves between such traditions as poetry, autobiography, philosophy, theology, and, of course, journalism—we can say that, on a very obvious level, *Let Us Now Praise Famous Men* is a book that consists of two heterogeneous parts: photographs by Walker Evans and text by James Agee. It is the collaborative result of two authors working in two media using two different instruments—"the motionless camera, and the printed word"—which are both subtended by, as Agee writes, the "governing instrument [of] . . . individual, anti-authoritative human consciousness."[1] But, if we remove the grammatical article from "work" and accentuate the verbal aspect of the word as verbal substantive, the question's pragmatic dimension comes to be favored. What kind of *work* is this book—that is, what kind of labor does it perform? In both generic and pragmatic terms, how do the two parts that constitute *Let Us Now Praise Famous Men* work together? What is the logic of their collaboration?

I pose these "work-related" questions of a book that is itself ostensibly guided by labor as its theme, a book whose topic is ostensibly the lives of cotton tenant farmers in the American South during the Depression. It might follow, then, that the way the authors carry out and divide the labor of their project would have some bearing on their treatment of the theme, and vice versa. I hope, in the following pages, to begin to unravel a few of the complex ways *Let Us Now Praise Famous Men* is implicated in its ostensible theme of work.

❧

Since it was first published in 1941, *Let Us Now Praise Famous Men* has been reissued several times, appearing in 2005 as a volume in the prestigious Library of America series. Curiously, despite this inclusion in the American equivalent of the Pléiades and the canonicity of several of Evans's photographs, the book remains relatively little-known outside certain circles— namely, historians of Depression America, students of documentary journalism, and postbellum Americanists—and still only verges on being accepted as a major classic text. A brief factual account of the inception, evolution, and early reception of the project may thus be in order here for those unfamiliar with the book.

The publication and reception history of this book is remarkable for its delays and surprising twists. The project originated in 1936 when *Fortune* magazine commissioned "a photographic and verbal account of cotton tenantry" that involved traveling to the Deep South and finding an "average" or "representative" family of white tenant farmers. The assignment was given to Agee, a *Fortune* staff writer since 1932 whose earlier article on the Tennessee Valley Authority had attracted the attention of the publisher, Henry Luce. Agee accepted the commission on the condition that he be paired with Evans instead of Margaret Bourke-White, who, as staff photographer, had been originally assigned to him. Evans was at the time working for the U.S. government as a photographer for the Farm Security Administration (FSA) (which also employed, besides Evans, such talents as Dorothea Lange and Ben Shahn) and was thus officially "on loan" from the government when he took the *Fortune* job.

He and Agee headed to Hale County, Alabama, in July 1936, where they found and lived for four weeks with not one but three related families, spending most of their time with one of them, the Burroughs, known in the book as "the Gudgers." After returning back up North, Agee finished a first version of the manuscript for *Fortune* in 1937. Ten times longer than what the editors expected, the work was deemed unpublishable. The publishing house Harper then paid Agee for a year off from his job to complete a second version of the manuscript. This version was completed in 1939 and also rejected after Agee refused the editors' suggestions of "deletions in the interests of good taste." The book, now over four hundred pages long, finally appeared with Houghton Mifflin in 1941, to mixed reviews.[2] Commercially, it flopped, selling a little over six hundred copies by the end of 1941 and going out of print in 1948 after selling only a little more than a thousand.

The book received new life in 1960. Agee had died in 1955 of a heart attack, and was posthumously awarded the Pulitzer Prize two years later for his unfinished novel *A Death in the Family*. In the wake of Agee's death and the Pulitzer, Houghton Mifflin decided to reissue *Let Us Now Praise Famous Men*. For this edition, Evans doubled the number of photographs to sixty-two and added a brief commemorative foreword, "James Agee in 1936." This time, the book was a major success, both critically and commercially, finding particular resonance with a new generation of educated, socially and politically progressive youth. Famously, it became a text that inspired and literally accompanied civil rights workers on their journeys to the rural South.[3] After a period of abeyance of almost twenty years, this book ostensibly about the plight of white tenant farmers during the Depression came back to find an audience, and, in a curious historical twist, to exert a practical impact on what might be considered the altogether-separate sphere of race relations.

To put it mildly, the work *Let Us Now Praise Famous Men* turned out to be was not the work the editors at *Fortune* had envisioned. To begin with, in terms of formal conventions, it did not resemble any of its predecessors or peers in social documentary. Ever since the pioneering work of Jacob Riis in the tenements of New York in the 1890s, the practice of combining photographs and text in documentary reportage had become well established. Photographic technology and magazine publication grew apace in a mutually enhancing relationship in the early decades of the twentieth century. In 1937, the same year Agee turned in the first version of his manuscript to *Fortune*, George Orwell's *The Road to Wigan Pier* was published in Britain, and the collaboration between the writer Erskine Caldwell and the photographer Margaret Bourke-White, *You Have Seen Their Faces*—which likewise documents poverty in the South—was published to much critical acclaim and commercial success in the United States.

Formally, *Let Us Now Praise Famous Men* differs from these examples in the way Evans's photographs are presented completely separate from Agee's text. They appear in a gallery right at the beginning of the book before the title page or any front matter whatsoever, unaccompanied by captions or any explanatory commentary. It is even suggested, in the 1941 edition, that the photographs constitute a book 1, in relation to which Agee's text follows as book 2.[4] About this format, Agee writes in the preface: "The photographs are not illustrative. They, and the text, are co-equal, mutually independent, and fully collaborative" (xi). This statement of equality and independence à propos the relationship between the two media, the two arts, carries with it unmistakable political overtones: how photographs and text relate to each other is of no less importance politically than what they attempt to show and narrate.

Agee reiterates in the first paragraph of his preface what *Fortune* expected of him and Evans: "It was our business to prepare, for a New York magazine, an article on cotton tenantry in the United States, in the form of a photographic and verbal record of the daily living and environment of an average white family of tenant farmers" (ix). A photographic and verbal record they did end up making, but it was one that constituted a critical interrogation and radical transformation of the premises of *Fortune*'s assignment. Beginning in the summer of 1936, Agee and Evans used this assignment as their point of departure for a bold and passionate experiment of profound aesthetic and political consequence. In Agee's words, they used the "nominal subject" of "North American cotton tenantry as examined in the daily living of three representative white tenant families" as their starting point for, above all, an "effort . . . to recognize the stature of a portion of unimagined existence, and to contrive techniques proper to its recording, communication, analysis, and defense" (xi).

What are the premises of the *Fortune* assignment? Agee reiterates not just in his preface but also throughout the text the publishing institution's demands for an "article on cotton tenantry" for which "representative" or "average" "tenant farmers" were to be found. Through these reiterations can be heard the powerful voice of the institutional authority that Agee and Evans refuse to extend and in fact tried to interrupt. *Fortune*'s commission for an article on cotton tenantry per se is predicated on the self-evident notion of the division of labor, a principle fundamental to the tradition of politics. In book 2 of Plato's *Republic*, Socrates asks his young auditors, "Tell me, then, . . . how our city will suffice for the provision of all these things. Will there not be a farmer for one, and a builder, and then again a weaver? And shall we add thereto a cobbler and some other purveyor for the needs of the body? . . . The indispensable minimum of a city, then, would consist of four or five men."[5] In dispatching Agee and Evans to the Deep South to bring back up North a report on those who grow cotton, *Fortune* is putting into operation this fundamental logic.

According to the principle of the division of labor, the state consists of a collectivity of citizens performing specific, circumscribed tasks who benefit from one another in so doing. In very broad terms, society in the age of industrial-capitalist modernity saw the growth of an increasingly differentiated division of labor, for which scientifically based management theories emerged to make the system's functioning ever more efficient. The dangers that accompany this efficiency have been famously articulated by thinkers as various as Adam Smith and Karl Marx, and such articulations include the atrophying of the creativity of individuals trained in only one skill, the alienation and commodification of labor from the creative human being, and the rise of a hierarchy of labor that perpetuates itself not through merit but by birth. Management, organization, and efficiency are values attached to the modern state viewed as a collectivity of occupations or professions; and, from this perspective, politics becomes indistinguishable from the telling and now-antiquated term "political economy."

It is in keeping with the division of labor that the journalist-writer and the FSA photographer were sent to Alabama in the summer of 1936 to report on the predicament of cotton tenant farmers. Why did *Fortune* want to publish such a report? What did the magazine aim to show, to make and transmit in visible and legible form? The trend for social documentary had grown during the years of the Depression, backed by both private organizations and governmental agencies. Both Henry Luce's magazines[6] and the FSA sponsored projects to show parts of the population—in terms of occupation and class—to other parts of the population; and, relatedly, to show parts of the nation to other parts of the nation. Both private journalism and the government aimed to generate through such projects sympathy from those higher up the hierarchy of occupations and professions for those lower down—the "underprivileged" or the "disadvantaged"—at a time of national economic crisis, when that hierarchy had begun to look more like a slide than a ladder. In geographical terms, these organizations aimed to promote the image of a unified nation, not unlike the process of piecing together a child's jigsaw puzzle map of the United States. Dovetailing the conception of society as a collectivity of occupations is the conception of the nation in terms of a cartographical whole.

To whom did *Fortune* want to show this record? Whom does journalism serve? The answer would seem to be tautological: why, the "reading public," of course. But what is this public? This reading public consists, in

effect, of those parts of the population that have the ability to read or to buy
Fortune, a reading public that excludes the tenant farmers, who are impover-
ished and, at best, semiliterate. The word "money" recurs as motif in the
second paragraph and second sentence of Agee's preamble, as he unfolds
gradually and systematically in one long, syntactically virtuosic prose poem
of a sentence the relationship between journalists, tenant farmers, and reading public, who are introduced in that order:

> It seems to me curious, not to say obscene and thoroughly terrifying that it
> could occur to an association of human beings drawn together through need
> and chance and for profit into a company, an organ of journalism, to pry
> intimately into the lives of an undefended and appallingly damaged group of
> human beings, an ignorant and helpless rural family, for the purpose of
> parading the nakedness, disadvantage and humiliation of these lives before
> another group of human beings, in the name of science, of "honest journal-
> ism" (whatever that paradox may mean), of humanity, of social fearlessness,
> for money, and for a reputation for crusading and for unbias which, when
> skillfully enough qualified, is exchangeable at any bank for money (and in
> politics, for votes, job patronage, abelincolnism, etc.*; and that these people
> could be capable of meditating this prospect without the slightest doubt of
> their qualification to do an "honest" piece of work, and with a conscience
> better than clear, and in the virtual certitude of almost unanimous public
> approval. (5)

In the last clause, the sentence returns to the journalists, who, if they
were to discharge this task as such, would be sure to bask in the "approval"
conferred on them by the public or, rather, conferred on them *in* public.
The adjective "public" near the end of the sentence would seem to describe
not so much the readers as a separate "group of human beings" as the
medium through which journalists and readers relate to each other, that
medium they share but that does not include the other "group of human
beings" known as "tenant farmers" or "sharecroppers." This medium of
the public is a rational sphere regulated by "science" in which progressive
benevolence and liberal compassion can take place, where "humanity" can
be staged for the purpose of spreading knowledge and promoting sympathy;
and the perpetuation of this sphere is sustained by the undercurrent of
money.

Agee performs an explicit assault on this version of the public for the rest
of the preamble. He addresses directly in the second person the reader qua

---

*Money. [Agee's footnote.]

member of this public when he asks, "Who are you who will read these words and study these photographs, and through what cause, by what chance, and for what purpose, and by what right do you qualify to, and what will you do about it . . . ?" Then he turns to himself and Evans, who are also members of such a public: "the question, Why we make this book, and set it at large, and by what right, and for what purpose, and to what good end, or none" (7). And what they will not do is create and circulate what he describes parodically as:

> a book about "sharecroppers," . . . written for all those who have a soft place in their hearts for the laughter and tears inherent in poverty viewed at a distance, and especially for those who can afford the retail price; in the hope that the reader will be edified, and may feel kindly disposed toward any well-thought-out liberal efforts to rectify the unpleasant situation down South, and will somewhat better and more guiltily appreciate the next good meal he eats; and in the hope, too, that he will recommend this little book to really sympathetic friends, in order that our publishers may at least cover their investment and that just the merest perhaps) some kindly thought may be turned our way, and a little of your money fall to poor little us. (11–12)

This passage is a thinly veiled description of the highly successful 1937 Caldwell–Bourke-White *You Have Seen Their Faces*, which Agee explicitly returns to when he pastes in the "Notes and Appendices" section newspaper articles on the glamorous Bourke-White in action. Agee and Evans need to create a record, invent a new mode of communication that does not mechanically repeat and participate in this version of the public.

In the tradition of politics, the notion of the public usually designates what is shared in a community, the domain in which citizens take part in the common. If, according to the division of labor, society consists of a collectivity of occupational identities, what is the relationship between the "public" and society as a collectivity of parts? Obviously, they are not congruent. Among contemporary thinkers, Jacques Rancière has devoted himself to rethinking what it means for the citizen of a democracy to take part in the common. In *The Politics of Aesthetics* he observes that, in the political tradition, the question of "who can have a share in what is common to the community [is] based on what they do and on the time and space in which this activity is performed. Having a particular 'occupation' thereby determines the ability or inability to take charge of what is common to the community; it defines what is visible or not in a common space, endowed with a common language, etc."[7] The sharecroppers as such have no share in the common, no share in the public: they function, in Agee's analysis, instead as the part excluded from the common that is necessarily and paradoxically included, however, for the very constitution of the common.

Rancière seeks in his critique of the political tradition to redefine on a radical level the very notion of the part, and the structure of the democratic citizen's taking part in the common. Genuine politics, genuine democracy, according to Rancière, happens only when a part separates from and opens up society conceived as a stable totality of parts. This part that separates he calls "the demos": "The demos is not the real totality or ideal totalisation of a human collectivity. Neither is it the masses as opposed to the elite. The demos is, instead, an abstract separation of a population from itself. It is a supplementary part over and above the sum of a population's parts. Political subjects are, thus, not representatives of parts of the population but processes of subjectivation which introduce a disagreement, a dissensus."[8]

The demos as part is not equivalent to any existing part of the population; it is instead an active force that rises and shows the non-totalizability of the system. It does not correspond to any existing group, such as the "share-croppers" or "landowners" or "journalists," but is precisely supplementary to all three categories. To become a political subject, according to Rancière, is not to speak for or as the member of a part of the population, construed as an occupational or ethnic or some other such identity, but rather is a dynamic process of activating dissensus. And political dissensus is not simply a conflict of interests, opinions, or values. It is a conflict over the common itself. It is not a quarrel over which solutions to apply to a situation but rather a dispute over the situation itself, a dispute over what is visible as an element of a situation, over which visible elements belong to what is common, over the capacity of subjects to designate this common and argue for it. Political dissensus is the division of perceptible givens themselves.[9]

Dissensus is irreducible to what Rancière calls the logic of "consensus," the dominant model of modern liberal democracy, which involves representatives of parts of the population speaking to one another in parliamentary fashion, reaching decisions on how to manage the whole. According to consensus, one has a part in the common, becomes a political subject, only by identifying with a preexisting part or division. In dissensus, on the other hand, emphasis should be placed on the verbal aspect of "division"— likewise on the verb "to part" in "part" (the *partager* in *partage*). Political dissensus is the *act* of dividing perceptible givens themselves, while consensus operates in accordance with given divisions. Dissensus redefines the parameters and transforms the very character of the common; consensus presupposes the common as given and perpetuates it as such.

In transforming the terms of the *Fortune* assignment, Agee and Evans refuse to deliver a report on the "sharecroppers" as one of the lowest within society's divisions of labor, to present them to those parts of the population that constitute the public. The authors do, however, heed the imperative to make a photographic and verbal record of their life with the families in Alabama, but the record they create is not a "documentary realist" record in mimetic conformity with the division of society into parts. This record is one that, to begin with, entails a rechristening of the sharecroppers. Thus their book is dedicated not to the "sharecroppers" or "tenant families," but "[t]o those of whom the record is made./In gratefulness and in love./J. A./ W. E." What the record shows is thus not "the sharecroppers" as a division of labor, nor "the poor" substantialized as a "class." Rather, what the record aims to bring to visibility and legibility, I contend, is precisely the supplemental part, that which emerges as supernumerary to the sum of all parts, an abstraction that prevents the collectivity from closing and totalizing itself. Agee and Evans try to invent a new mode of communication, to transform the parameters of the common, and to address a community irreducible to society considered in terms of the division of labor.[10] In this process, political subjects constitute themselves by separating from their representative categories: the authors do not report as journalist/governmental employees, those of whom they tell become something other than sharecroppers, and the reader-viewer is addressed as something other than a member of the "reading public." In this sense, *Let Us Now Praise Famous Men* is a collective effort "in which," as Agee writes, "the reader is no less centrally involved than the authors and those of whom they tell" (xi).

Thus this book that starts out as a report on cotton tenantry swerves away from thematizing agricultural labor. Commentators Janis Bergman-Carton and Evan Carton summarize how, "though both artists witnessed and recorded the tenants' domestic routines, agricultural labors, and social and familial interactions, *Let Us Now Praise Famous Men*, in word and in image, represents such activities minimally, if at all."[11]

In the 1941 edition, none of Evans's thirty-one photographs shows any member of the families working in the field (i.e., as a sharecropper per se); in the 1960 edition, only one newly inserted image among the sixty-two photographs shows someone working, an image curious for its resemblance to a painting by Jean-François Millet. Agee's text contains a section titled "Work," but he relegates it to a peripheral position within the overall structure, suggesting that work is only one aspect, rather than the determining factor, in the record he makes. Displacing their "nominal subject" of "cotton tenantry," Agee and Evans aim instead to "recognize the stature of a portion of unimagined existence, and to contrive techniques proper to its recording, communication, analysis, and defense" (x). What strategies do they employ to invent a new mode of communication beyond the logic of the division of labor? How do they transform the parameters of the common?

Let us return briefly to the generic questions raised at the beginning of the chapter. *Let Us Now Praise Famous Men* is a book that consists of two parts. How are we to think of the relationship between them? In the preface, Agee asserts, "The photographs are not illustrative. They, and the text, are co-equal, mutually independent, and fully collaborative" (xi). How are we to understand this statement of equality and independence in collaboration? Critics have generally interpreted the relationship between the parts as "contrastive or contrapuntal," using a critical vocabulary that combines formal terms with moral-psychological judgments.[12] Evans's photographs are "objective," "straightforward," "restrained," "impersonal," "respectful"— terms that correspond roughly to such formal features as clarity, frontality, preference for the middle distance, and the avoidance of candid, stop-action shots in favor of posed, eye-level portraits. Agee's prose is "subjective," "digressive," "self-indulgent," "effusive"—terms that correspond roughly to nonlinearity of narrative and frequent attention to the writer as mediating agent. Evans was "secular," Agee "religious." Such comparisons bespeak a humanistic logic of "aesthetic sensibility" or temperament, according to which the authors function as two separate but equal artists who offer two distinct perspectives in the records they make. *Let Us Now Praise Famous Men* would then consist of two parallel records, placed side by side between the covers of one book.

What upsets this humanistic logic, which treats the two parts as equal emanations of two artists who function as integral, unitary parts, is precisely the incommensurability of the two media of communication. Agee names the two immediate instruments involved in making the record—"the motionless camera, and the printed word"—and the media to which they correspond would be the visual medium and the textual medium. Evans, working with the camera in the visual medium, privileges the sense of sight, the domain of the visible. Agee, working with words in the textual medium, appeals to both sight and hearing, to the relationship between the visible and the audible. Part of what the photographic record shows is necessarily unavailable to the textual medium, and part of what the textual record shows is necessarily missing from the visual. The question of the relationship between the two parts of the text—and the equality and independence of the collaboration—needs to be thought, then, in terms of the incommensurability of the media rather than in terms of authorial identity.

The Photographic Record

What kind of intervention in the visual domain do Evans's photographs constitute? What and how does the photographic record communicate in a new way? To begin with, let us review the images in their sequential arrangement. Many of the photographs Evans took in Hale County, Alabama, have been reproduced and given different connotations in numerous other contexts; several of them have attained the status of classics in the history of photography. The portrait of Ellie Mae Burroughs, known in the book as "Annie Mae Gudger," especially ranks alongside Dorothea Lange's "Migrant Mother" as one of the most famous images from the Depression. But in both the 1941 and 1960 editions of *Let Us Now Praise Famous Men*, these detachable images are arranged in specific sequences that encourage the viewer to project particular interpretations.[13]

What a quick slide show viewing of both the 1941 and 1960 versions shows is a feudal, patriarchal system. The first image the viewer encounters in both versions is the three-quarter portrait of a landlord figure, re-cropped to lessen the background and bring him closer to the viewer in the 1960 edition. We know he is a landlord because he is well-groomed and wearing a linen jacket and seersucker pants, hallmarks of southern gentility; and he is standing against the backdrop of a clapboard wall, looking warily at the camera. Images of three families follow next, presented family by family. Each familial unit begins with an individual portrait of the patriarch— named in the book Gudger, Woods, and Ricketts—before it shows images of the wife/mother and the children. Each family unit includes portraits of ragged, malnourished individuals—adults and children—as well as group portraits; and they include shots of interior spaces as well as exterior views of the houses the families inhabit.

After the families, the sequence shows images of the nearby town and environs—only three in 1941, expanded to nineteen in 1960—including roads, streets, and the exteriors of institutional buildings. Both sequences move from country to town, from familial to public space. The 1941 version especially reinforces the feudal interpretation. Beginning with the image of the landlord standing sentinel against the wall, it ends with an image of the mayor's office with jail upstairs (see Figure 1). Evans satirizes the pomposity of provincial power in this image by positioning the camera frontally in a way that flattens the building and makes it appear like a two-dimensional facade in a movie set. And he sets the camera at just the right distance to capture clearly the building's reflection, along with the inverted words "Mayor's Office," in a puddle on the dirt road in the foreground—a parody of touristic images of European lakeside castles, as well as the *reflet dans l'eau* type of art photograph made popular by photo-secessionism.[14]

The 1960 edition maintains this basic sequencing but introduces a few changes. Several portraits are re-cropped to bring the human figures closer to the viewer, and a few images in the family sections are replaced. The greatest expansion comes, of course, in the town and environs section, where the original three images of Main Street, abandoned storefronts, and the mayor's office are interspersed between images of schools, more stores,

Figure 1. Walker Evans, "Moundville, Alabama. Mayor's office." (Farm Security Administration. U.S. Library of Congress Prints and Photographs Division.)

a post office/gas station, a railroad station, a boarding house, and a barber shop, among other scenes. The effect is like that of a "zooming out" on the map. Evans shows in his reedited sequence the connections of the families to a wider, more intricate political and economic system. In fact, several of the images he inserted in 1960 were not even taken in Hale County but in Birmingham and, across state lines, in Vicksburg, Mississippi. These changes could be explained away by what is popularly called "historical hindsight." From the vantage point of 1960, Evans offers in the reedited sequence more glimpses of roads and cars, indicating the rise of an automobile culture; more images of African Americans, underlining a racially mixed South; more Coca Cola signs, suggesting the rise of a particularly southern, soon-to-become multinational conglomerate, along with the spread of advertising as a dominant form of image making. The altered sequence suggests a displacement of feudalism by capitalism.

These sequencings certainly invite a sociological-anthropological reading, but we do not view photographs merely as a succession of frames in a moving slide show. If we review the images more slowly, pausing between them, they resemble less a diachronic narrative than a poetic sequence, such as a sonnet cycle or collection of prose poems. Each frame is a synchronic composition that complicates and problematizes a diachronic reading and can be approached according to an alternative taxonomy: portraits of adults, portraits of children, group portraits, landscapes, building exteriors, signs, and so forth. A closer look at instances of such topoi problematizes generalizations that are possible in a sweeping topographical survey. Among the topoi Evans uses, I consider more closely now one in particular: his images of the fireplace. There are two fireplace images in the 1941 edition, both taken in the Gudger house. Evans retains only one of these in the 1960 edition (see Figure 2), but he adds an image of a defunct fireplace (see Figure 3) and another of a working fireplace, both in the Ricketts home (see Figure 4).

One remarkable feature about these particular images is that there are corresponding passages in Agee's text that describe them in such ekphrastic detail that they could be considered extended captions. Throughout his text, Agee refers to Evans, reconstructing scenarios in which Evans was taking photographs; and, in other passages, he reflects more abstractly on the medium of photography. The reader is likely, while reading the text, to flip back to the images to identify faces and places, but it is only with these particular images and nowhere else in the collaboration that there emerges a convergence between images and text. I include below a few excerpts from these lengthy passages, which occur in the structural-chronological

Figure 2. Walker Evans, "Fireplace and wall detail in bedroom of Floyd Burroughs's cabin. Hale County, Alabama." (Farm Security Administration. U.S. Library of Congress Prints and Photographs Division.)

center of the text, in the section titled "Shelter." Apropos the Gudger fireplace (Figure 2), Agee writes:

> On the mantel against the glowing wall, each about six inches from the ends
> of the shelf, two small twin vases, very simply blown, of pebble-grained iri-
> descent glass. Exactly at center between them, a fluted saucer, with a coarse
> lace edge, of pressed milky glass, which Louise's mother gave her to call her
> own and for which she cares more dearly than for anything else she possesses.
> Pinned all along the edge of this mantel, a broad fringe of white tissue pat-
> tern-paper which Mrs. Gudger folded many times on itself and scissored into
> pierced geometrics of lace, and of which she speaks as her last effort to make
> this house pretty. . . .
>   At the right of the mantel, in whitewash, all its whorlings sharp, the print
> of a child's hand. (143, 145)

Apropos the defunct Ricketts fireplace (Figure 3):

> Several of the windowpanes are broken out and though some of these are
> stopped with rags and with squares of cardboard, that is not enough: for the
> whole rear wall of the fireplace is burst through, letting in a large hole of
> daylight, and the stone chimney has fallen in on itself. . . . At the center of
> the stone chimney, between two windows, and in line above the stove-in
> tunnel of bright gasping country, hang a hat and a sign. The hat is round,
> and is homemade of brilliant cornshucks. The sign is made on the smooth
> side of a rectangle of corrugated cardboard, in blue crayon, part in print and
> part in a lopside running hand . . . (173)

And, matching the image of the second, working Ricketts fireplace (Figure
4), Agee writes:

> The Ricketts are much more actively fond of pretty things than the other
> families are, and have lived here longer than they have, and in obedience of
> these equations the fireplace wall is crusted deep with attractive pieces of
> paper into the intricate splendor of a wedding cake or the fan of a white
> peacock: calendars of snowbound and stag-hunting scenes pressed into bas-
> relief out of white pulp and glittering with a sand of red and blue and green
> and gold tinsel, and delicately tinted; other calendars and farm magazine cov-
> ers or advertisements of dog-love . . . (174–5)

We know from the narrative portions of the text framing these ekphrastic
descriptions that Agee and Evans were present together before these fireplaces and walls, the former taking notes and the latter taking photographs.

Figure 3. Walker Evans, "Cotton room, formerly prayer meeting room. Frank Tengle's farm. Hale County, Alabama." (Farm Security Administration. U.S. Library of Congress Prints and Photographs Division.)

Figure 4. Walker Evans, "Fireplace in Frank Tengle's home. Hale County, Alabama." (Farm Security Administration. U.S. Library of Congress Prints and Photographs Division.)

But the mere fact of the two bodies being in the same room at the same time does not explain the mutuality of attentiveness to this particular manifestation of the lives of the farmers. Who taught whom to see and pay attention in this way—the writer or the photographer? The question of priority may not be decidable in any definitive way, but the point is that both writer and photographer make the humble hearth of the lowly an object of communal attention.

What is a fireplace? As its synonym "hearth" connotes, the fireplace is a traditional symbol of the home, the *oikos*, the private as distinguished from the public. Both writer and photographer bring to public visibility this symbol of private space. That these fireplaces are built into walls, rather than say, pits, makes it possible for them also to be something else—namely, sites that provide a decorative surface. The mantelpiece serves, in the modern home, as a quasi-museum for the family, alongside the dresser or the dressing table. The descriptions of both Agee and Evans allow us to see the fireplaces as murals where the members of the families produce collages, where they themselves produce isolatable images. In so doing, Agee and Evans may display here affinities with earlier writers and photographers: in the literary tradition, Flaubert's description of Félicité's room at the end of *Un coeur simple* comes to mind; in the visual, Evans's distinct influence here is also French, Eugéne Atget.

Atget is now considered one of the major figures of the history of photography, an inaugurator of "realistic," "vernacular," "documentary" style, but he worked in obscurity until his death in 1927. His photographs of Paris had gone unappreciated, unrecognized, and literally unseen until the American photographer Berenice Abbott published them posthumously in 1930 in the volume *Atget: Photographe de Paris*. Evans had spent the years 1926–7 in Paris, where, like other Americans of his generation, he had gone as a young man aspiring to become a writer after such models as Flaubert and Baudelaire. There, he started taking pictures.

As a photographer, he came to define his style in contradistinction to, on the one hand, the dominant trend of art photography associated with Alfred Stieglitz and, on the other, a rising commercial photography associated with Edward Steichen. He writes against both these trends in the 1931 essay "The Reappearance of Photography," in which Atget emerges as the principal exponent of the essay's title. What Evans has to say there about Atget applies to his own developing style as well: "Apparently he was oblivious to everything but the necessity of photographing Paris and its environs; but just what vision he carried in him of the monument he was leaving is not clear. It is possible to read into his photographs so many things he may never have formulated to himself . . . His general note is lyrical understanding of the street, trained observation of it, special feeling for patina, eye for revealing detail . . ."[15]

In Atget's photographs of the streets and scenes of Paris, which he himself had seen, Evans saw a practice specific to the medium of photography, a descriptive observation of the visible world that did not, like art photography, take its cues from painting. Atget the flaneur photographed Paris as he saw without interfering with the seen, without moving objects around to create visual compositions. He left the studio for the street, and he trained his eye to perceive patterns in everyday urban modernity. For Evans, photography and the world visible outside the studio reappeared together through Atget.

Atget repeatedly photographed Parisian shopwindows (Figure 5), as well as the interiors of working-class homes (Figure 6). Thematically and stylistically, such images are precursors of Evans's fireplace photographs for *Let Us Now Praise Famous Men*. What Atget discovered in Paris in the arcade windows visible from the street and the domestic interiors were readymade showcases, vitrines of everyday life, collections of objects people display and that suggest something about how people assemble the visual. But it took Atget's eye and his camera to transform such everyday sights into an image on a two-dimensional plane: the process of "creating," paradoxically speaking, the objet trouvé. In New York Evans had started taking photographs of shopwindows and signs in the late 1920s, and already, in the early 1930s before arriving in Alabama, he had started taking photographs of working-class interiors and would continue to do so after Alabama. Commenting in a 1971 interview on an image he had made in 1945 of a dressing table in Biloxi, Mississippi (Figure 7), Evans says:

> This shows what I call "unconscious arrangement." It's a kind of eternal theme, though I'd never seen it done. Again, it's something I collected. You've got to collect. This is a piece of the anatomy of somebody's living. . . . I was visiting Biloxi. Greek fishermen, shrimp fishermen, lived nearby. Their homes were all together. A friend got me inside. The artist gets rewarded by finding a thing like this. You know that people haven't seen this this way, and here you're able to show it to them, to say "Look at this with me, look at the expression of the value of pictures, the instinctive joy in pictures this dressing table shows." The great simple appeal of the *picture*, here it is among Greek fishermen, decorating their house with love and excitement, and plain direct pleasure.[16]

Figure 5. Eugène Atget, "Marché du temple."

Figure 6. Eugène Atget, "Chambre à coucher."

Figure 7. Walker Evans, "Bedroom dresser, shrimp fisherman's house. Biloxi, Mississippi." (© Walker Evans Archive, The Metropolitan Museum of Art.)

Like Duchamp, Atget and Evans practiced an art of the objet trouvé, collected them in their image making. But the object found and transformed into art is, unlike a urinal or a bicycle wheel, an assemblage created by others. This assemblage was not made on any conscious level to be viewed as "art" but, in the very everyday unconsciousness of arranging, reveals something about how human beings see and relate to images.

In his fireplace photographs for *Let Us Now Praise Famous Men*, Evans brought his vision for such "unconscious arrangements," an eye trained in the streets of Paris and New York as well as rural homes in upstate New York and West Virginia, to the homes of the tenant farmers. These images do not show the sharecroppers qua sharecroppers—as would a picture of them picking cotton or tilling the field—but reveal them in their absence as image makers. In stylistic and technical terms, these fireplace photographs are "Evansian" in a signature way. He positioned his eight-by-ten-view camera frontally to capture descriptive detail and give as much factual information about the farmers' choices as possible. A flash was used to facilitate this descriptive clarity. The two images of the working fireplaces themselves have a flatness about them that resonates with Evans's general interest in the wall as a two-dimensional surface that presents visible as well as legible information. Evans achieves this flatness by excluding any angles of the room that would show the wall's connectedness to other planes.

Evans was a lifelong collector and photographer of signs—traffic signs, advertising signs, and so forth—and it is this fascination with the two-dimensional surface that sets him apart from Atget. He was uniquely interested in the visuality of mass-produced, legible, printed matter, such as the calendars and journal covers the Gudgers and the Ricketts use to decorate their walls, which simultaneously advertise doctor's offices, shoe stores, and medicines. On the pages of the book, these fireplace photographs are, of course, themselves two-dimensional images that, in turn, reveal how the Gudgers and the Ricketts participate through images in public life and appropriate them by detaching these images from their commercial contexts. Through these photographs Evans shares with the viewer his seeing of others' seeing. Perhaps the most suitable captions for them would be: "Look at this with me, look at the expression of the value of pictures" these fireplaces show.

At these sites in the Gudger and Ricketts homes Evans discovers "unconscious arrangements" that, through the photographic process, he brings to public consciousness, in the sense of making them visible to viewers previously unable even to see such aspects of the world as part of the common.

In conclusion, I return to the image of the defunct Ricketts fireplace (Figure 3), which, unlike the other two images, does not show the fireplace as a site of decoration per se. What this image shows is literally a camera obscura. The misspelled sign hanging above the hat serves as an excellent caption for this allegory of Evans's photographic practice in *Let Us Now Praise Famous Men*: "Please be quite. Every body is welcome."

The Written Record

I turn now to Agee's text, which, in concert with Evans's photographs, attempts to invent a new mode of communication, to transform the parameters of the common, and to address a community irreducible to society considered in terms of the division of labor.

The text is sui generis. It is nonlinear in exposition and presents out of chronological order events that took place during the visit to Alabama. It moves between multiple genres, modes, and techniques of both literary and nonliterary derivation—including poetry, drama, autobiography, philosophy, theology, scholarly annotation, inventory, aphorism, and collage. The analogy Agee uses to figure the movement of his narrative is, significantly, music. He organizes his text in a variation of sonata form, with three main sections joined by interludic material and characterized throughout by recurrent motifs. To the reader he recommends that his text be read not silently but aloud: "It is suggested that the reader attend with his ear to what he takes off the page: for variations of tone, pace, shape, and dynamics are here particularly unavailable to the eye alone, and with their loss, a good deal of meaning escapes" (xi).

The listening he demands of the reader is not a polite one, as at a concert in an auditorium, but an intense and wounding experience. Against any expectation that what the reader hears will be respectable "Art," he proposes this experiment:

> Get a radio or a phonograph capable of the most extreme loudness possible, and sit down to listen to a performance of Beethoven's Seventh Symphony or of Schubert's C-Major Symphony. . . . Get down on the floor and jam your ear as close into the loudspeaker as you can get it and stay there . . . Concentrate everything you can into your hearing and your body. You won't hear it nicely. If it hurts you, be glad of it. As near as you will ever get, you are inside the music; not only inside it, you are it; your body is no longer your shape and substance, it is the shape and substance of the music. (12–3)

This listening registers an impact not just on the ear but, through the sense of hearing, the sense of touch, for the placement of the eardrum on, against, into the loudspeaker, membrane against membrane, makes hearing indistinguishable from touch, the sense that engages the four other senses and therewith the entire body.[17] In such listening, all the senses are in communication with one another and with the object of perception. Agee aims to occasion in the reader a losing and refinding of the senses in the plural through addressing his prose to the ear, which, as he reminds the reader, opens up to what the eye alone cannot discern.

In so doing, he puts into question the traditional status of vision as sovereign among the senses, in conformity with the privileging of the intelligible over the sensible in the metaphysical view of the human.[18] Of course, Agee is not just substituting hearing for vision in the governing position but enacting a more radical revolution of the senses, in which the relationship of the senses to one another receives new articulation and the world as realm of appearances is not simply schematized as inferior and subordinate to a world beyond the world of "true reality."[19] In the task of writing about his encounter with the tenant families, Agee undertakes on more than one level, then, an *aesthetic* revolution. The world that emerges in his text is not a realm of the sensible that can be stabilized as finite and therefore "made sense of" from an external position. Rather, his text intervenes in the world as a world of appearances infinitely and unpredictably open to the possibility of change.

I follow the musical movement of Agee's text by studying several key moments. If this text follows sonata form, it initiates this structure right away in the series of epigraphs that constitute, after the preface, the second of the text's multiple thresholds. As the first cross section of the text, the epigraphs anticipate thematically, structurally, and stylistically much of what will follow in the next four-hundred-plus pages. They suggest already the erudition and allusiveness Agee will demonstrate throughout the book, with references ranging from the Bible to Beethoven to Freud, Céline, and Faulkner. The epigraphs are printed separately on consecutive pages and consist, respectively, of Lear's soliloquy on the heath, his famous address to the "poor naked wretches"; the last two sentences of Marx and Engels's *Communist Manifesto*; and the opening sentences from an early twentieth-century American children's geography textbook, *Around the World with the Children*, that belonged to the ten-year-old daughter of one of the tenant farmers. Each epigraph represents a different historical period, spanning early modernity to the author's present—the Renaissance, the nineteenth century, the twentieth century; a different generation in the course of human life—old age, middle age, childhood; and a different genre or discursive tradition—tragedy, political manifesto, contemporary children's textbook.

For reasons of space, I will not reproduce these epigraphs as they appear on separate pages, diminishing somewhat the dramatic force Agee's presentation gives them, but simply in successive order here:

Poor naked wretches, whereso'er you are,
That bide the pelting of this pitiless storm,
How shall your houseless heads and unfed sides,
Your loop'd and window'd raggedness, defend you
From seasons such as these? O! I have ta'en
Too little care of this! Take physick, pomp;
Expose thyself to feel what wretches feel,
That thou may'st shake the superflux to them,
And show the heavens more just.
★ ★ ★

Workers of the world, unite and fight. You have nothing to lose but your chains, and a world to win.
★ ★ ★

1. The Great Ball on Which We Live

The world is our home. It is also the home of many, many other children, some of whom live in far-away lands. They are our world brothers and sisters. . . .

2. Food, Shelter, and Clothing

What must any part of the world have in order to be a good home for man? What does every person need in order to live in comfort? Let us imagine that we are far out in the fields. The air is bitter cold and the wind is blowing. Snow is falling, and by and by it will turn into sleet and rain. We are almost naked. We have had nothing to eat and are suffering from hunger as well as cold. Suddenly the Queen of the Fairies floats down and offers us three wishes.

What shall we choose?

"I shall wish for food, because I am hungry," says Peter.

"I shall choose clothes to keep out the cold," says John.

"And I shall ask for a house to shelter me from the wind, the snow, and the rain," says little Nell with a shiver.

Now everyone needs food, clothing, and shelter. The lives of most men on earth are spent in getting these things. In our travels we shall wish to learn what our world brothers and sisters eat, and where their food comes from. We shall wish to see the houses they dwell in and how they are built. We shall wish also to know what clothing they use to protect themselves from the heat and the cold.[20]

In a footnote to the second epigraph, Agee explicitly refers to sonata form as the principle organizing the juxtaposition of epigraphs, and boldly disclaims affiliation with any specific political party agenda.[21] The widely divergent quotations of this opening sequence anticipate the generic hybridity of the text; and the way they are put into resonant counterpoint with each other, as in an overture, suggests the way the narration will depart from a linear expository structure.

What do these quotations of widely different provenance have in common? What emerges as resonant in their juxtaposition? What each of them does, in common with the others, I claim, is to put "the world" into question in the face of the unknown. Driven from Goneril's house, Lear enters the heath as a place of abandonment and exile, an inhospitable landscape where human beings are exposed to the elements. The king is in exile in the kingdom over which he once presided, and here he apostrophizes the "poor naked wretches" who had escaped his purview before and figure the *outside* of his sovereign jurisdiction to which he now desires to expose himself.

At the end of *The Communist Manifesto*, Marx and Engels apostrophize the "workers of the world" to constitute themselves as a unity and to fight for change: what is at stake is the "world" itself—which is not, at the moment of address, self-evident as their home but somehow alienated, yet to be achieved. At the moment of exhortation, "nothing" belongs to the workers but their chains: ahead of them is the world as possibility.

The beginning of the third epigraph, the excerpt from the children's geography textbook, resonates uncannily with the last sentences from the *Communist Manifesto*: "The world is our home. It is also the home of many, many other children, some of whom live in far-away lands. They are our world brothers and sisters. . . ." The didactic adult speaker here states reassuringly that the "world" is a home that "we" inhabit with a plurality of other children. The textbook aims to expose the child-reader as member of this "we" to the unknown other children living in faraway parts of the globe. Interestingly, within this children's book excerpt, a version of Lear's situation on the heath is enacted, as Peter, John, and Nell are imaginarily exposed on the fields to wish for—and thus to wish to *learn*, to *see*, and to *know*—what the other children may need in order to inhabit the world as home.

In each of the epigraphs, either the speaker or the addressee is on the border of the unknown, on the verge of experiencing the world, once familiar, as strange—the precondition for, precisely, a reconstitution of the world. Each epigraph is thus in more than one sense a threshold text: threshold texts in themselves as well as situated at the very threshold of the book *Let Us Now Praise Famous Men*. Lear; Marx and Engels, and the workers they call on; the adult narrator as travel guide and his child addressees are all poised at the point of departure on a literal or figurative voyage, an adventure beyond the boundaries of the familiar. The speakers imagine or call on their addressees to imagine, at this transitional juncture, a condition of exposure or abandonment—in which the human being is stripped bare of trappings and possessions and has nothing to lose.

From Jacobean England to twentieth-century America, the epigraphs span the extent of modernity. In what way does *Let Us Now Praise Famous Men* follow these three modern efforts to face the world anew and reclaim it as home? It would seem that Agee finds in these quotations—which themselves resonate with one another—resonance with his and Evans's efforts in undertaking this project and creating this book for the reader. Lear's speech might seem to speak for the authors' experience as well as their ambition in publishing this record of their 1936 trip to Alabama: finding themselves exposed to a topography outside their safe world, they aim likewise to expose the reader to such unfamiliar territory, for the purpose of promoting compassion and "showing the heavens more just."

Agee follows up the epigraph from *King Lear* with the two others, which might be taken likewise to speak for the authors' experience and their ambition. But his footnote to the second epigraph detaches the cited words from affiliation with "any political party, faith, or faction"—with any stable position backed by an institution that would guarantee the meaning of the text. The words "mean not what the reader may care to think they mean, but what they say. . . . In the pattern of the work as whole, they are, in the sonata form, the second theme; the poetry facing them is the first." The figure of music emerges here to mark the very disjunction between meaning and saying, as a movement of excess that expropriates the cited words from affiliation with any group or institution and that exposes the meaning determined accordingly as incomplete. Agee's "musical" use of these quotations ex-scribes them from their particular contexts of authority to make them gestures in the movement of his text, gestures that the text itself will, beyond obediently repeating and resuming, powerfully renew.

King, philosophers, pedagogue—each imagines and seeks to ground the human being in the condition of having nothing, and belies in this pattern a view of the human as qualified by the condition of having and potentially disqualifiable from the common in terms of a not-having. While deploring a situation in which members of a democracy work to subsist, Agee will try in his text to go beyond seeing and representing the tenant farmers in terms of have-nots toward relating to them, more radically, as fellow human beings who themselves always already inhabit a shared world of speech and action, and are capable of disclosing themselves to others and of disclosing the other to himself. Agee will not just turn his gaze on the tenant farmers but will also struggle to communicate how his gaze has been surprised and transformed in its encounter with the gaze of others.

His struggle takes place not over the four weeks of 1936 but in the process of five years of writing. The text conveys through its musical form the *process* of this struggle; that is, it does not impart the conclusion of this struggle but communicates its very process in disclosure to the reader as addressee. I elaborate on this process as a movement from the experience of shame to the possibility of *praise*, the central speech act announced in the title of the book. Let us pause, before proceeding further, at yet another of the text's thresholds, where Agee refers once again to *King Lear* as point of departure for the journey of his text.

This time, Agee refers to the character of Edgar as alter ego for himself and Evans in the summer of 1936. In his "Dedicatory Verses to Evans," he writes:

> Against time and the damages of the brain
> Sharpen and calibrate. Not yet in full,
> Yet in some arbitrated part
> Order the façade of the listless summer.
>
> Spies, moving delicately among the enemy,
> The younger sons, the fools,
> Set somewhat aside the dialects and the stained skins of feigned madness,
> Ambiguously signal, baffle, the eluded sentinel.
>
> Edgar, weeping for pity, to the shelf of that sick bluff,
> Bring your blind father, and describe a little;

Behold him, part wakened, fallen among field flowers shallow
But undisclosed, withdraw.

Not yet that naked hour when armed,
Disguise flung flat, squarely we challenge the fiend.
Still, comrade, the running of beasts and the ruining heaven
Still captive the old wild king.

While the poem appears to recall the "listless summer" of 1936, it is written, curiously, in the present tense and the imperative mode. The speaker begins by addressing an indeterminate addressee, speaking as if he were outside of the scene evoked but, in the last stanza, enters the scene to form part of the "we." These enigmatic verses resemble stage directions, in which the speaker is both director and actor, the addressee another actor, with both speaker and addressee playing Edgar, who famously plays not himself but other parts while internally exiled in the kingdom. The theme of theatricality in this poem resonates with the list of "Persons and Places" Agee had presented in the form of dramatis personae, in which he had earlier listed himself and Evans as "spy" and "counter-spy," respectively "traveling as writer" and "photographer."

By casting Evans and himself in *King Lear*, Agee remembers the confused theatricality of that summer, during which identities were suspended and disclosure deferred—interestingly, the ambiguous "[b]ut undisclosed" in the last line of the third stanza could modify both "Edgar" and "blind father." It was a summer when the actors did not expose themselves to those around them. "Not yet," the poem repeats in its first and last stanzas, echoing Edgar's language of patience in the tragedy. But exposure will take place belatedly, as Agee reviews the events of that summer retrospectively in his text. Contrary to Edgar's progress in *King Lear*, however, *Let Us Now Praise Famous Men* will move through exposure toward praise instead of revenge, toward the future as unlimited and open, rather than one that remains dictated by the horizon of the past.

Agee foregrounds periodically throughout his text the process of his own composition. I call attention to a significant mention of Agee's writing that comes not from himself but Evans, who breaks his habitual silence in his foreword to the book's 1960 edition, "James Agee in 1936." The photographer, who was more comfortable remaining behind the scenes, uses his pen to commemorate his dead friend and collaborator and to include him, as an image, among those of Ellie Mae Burroughs, Floyd Burroughs, and others in the preceding gallery. In this verbal portrait, Evans writes: "Night was his time. In Alabama he worked I don't know how late. Some parts of *Let Us Now Praise Famous Men* read as though they were written on the spot at night. Later, in a small house in Frenchtown, New Jersey, the work, I think, was largely night-written. Literally the result shows this; some of the sections read best at night, far in the night. The first passage of *A Country Letter* . . . is particularly night-permeated" (vi). These remarks shed light also on a crucial distinction between the practitioners of the two media: night was Agee's time for writing; as Agee makes explicit in the passage Evans cites as well as throughout the text, night was when the record was made. As the photographs so starkly show, day was Evans's time for seeing and making images.

As the etymology of the word suggests, photography is an art that depends on light. There are many photographers who make nighttime images, of course, but Evans was one who preferred the visibility and clarity of the world that appeared in natural light. He took his photographs during the day, making as much use of natural light as possible, using a flash only when necessary inside the farmers' houses. The portraits were taken with the full awareness and consent of the subjects: they are neither candids nor studio portraits but encounters with the subjects against the backdrop of their homes.

Agee recounts often in his text Evans setting up equipment and himself helping to "get the camera ready." The photographer's activity of daytime record making has a definite chronological priority to Agee's nocturnal writing. And the indexicality of the photographic image serves to convey to the viewer a sense of the hic et nunc—of the photographer's having been *there* at *that* time in front of *these* people to make the images. In writing at night while others slept, Agee cannot reproduce this effect of immediacy. During the day, he was too busy *not* writing, participating in all the affairs of others that must take place during the day. The only hic et nunc that the writer can convey is that of himself writing. In counterpoint to Evans's photography of day, Agee's is a writing of night.

After the preamble there follows a page with no other words but "The house had now descended/All over Alabama the lamps are out." These lines form a refrain early in the text, calling attention to the situation of the writer. When the lamps go out, writing begins, figured as a kind of descent into the underworld.[22] Writing begins with the suspension of the everyday world, its unavailability to sensory perception:

The house and all that was in it had now descended deep beneath the gradual spiral it had sunk through; it lay formal under the order of entire silence. In the square pine room at the back the bodies of the man of thirty and of his wife and of their children lay on shallow mattresses on their iron beds and on the rigid floor, and they were sleeping, and the dog lay asleep in the hallway. Most human beings, most animals and birds who live in the sheltering ring of human influence, and a great portion of all the branched tribes of living in earth and air and water upon a half of the world, were stunned with sleep. (17)

"All over Alabama, the lamps are out," Agee repeats and imagines the world at rest that he cannot see, "The roads lie there, with nothing to use them. The fields lie there, with nothing at work in them, neither man nor beast" (41). In this darkness, writing begins with the light cast by a solitary lamp:

It is late in a summer night, in a room of a house set deep and solitary in the country; all in this house save myself are sleeping; I sit at a table, facing a partition wall; and I am looking at a lighted coal-oil lamp which stands on the table close to the wall, and just beyond the sleeping of my relaxed left hand; with my right hand I am from time to time writing, with a soft pencil, into a school-child's composition book; but just now, I am entirely focused on the lamp, and light. (44)

This passage begins the section titled "A Country Letter" that Evans cites above. Agee depicts himself here in a situation reminiscent of Descartes in the first of his *Meditations*, who thinks at first he cannot doubt that hic et nunc, while writing, "I am sitting here next to the fire, wearing my winter dressing gown, that I am holding this sheet of paper in my hands, and the like."[23] But even this situation, based on data he receives through his senses, will be subject to the madness of his doubt, for how many times has he not dreamt of being in such circumstances, "clothed in my dressing gown, seated next to the fireplace"?[24] He finds that he can overcome his doubt concerning his existence, preliminary to overcoming his doubt concerning the existence of the world and others in it, by ascertaining that he thinks. In his *Second Meditation*, Descartes formulates cogito, ergo sum as the discovery of his Archimedean point.

Agee likewise calls attention and returns to the hic et nunc of the scene of writing—be it in Alabama or Frenchtown, New Jersey—at night when the world is remote from the senses and the process of relating to it anew can begin. For Descartes, this process yields a new foundation for the sciences, at the center of which is the definition of the human as thinking subject, capable of *knowing* the world, for whom the chief problem to be overcome is doubt. For Agee, the problem that confronts him at night and needs to be overcome is not doubt but shame. Shame eludes the facades of the day but emerges in the textual medium of *Let Us Now Praise Famous Men* as the occasion for Agee's protracted reflections and attempts to relate to the world anew.

While doubt does not require the presence of others, shame essentially does. The Cartesian resolution of doubt in the cogito takes place in the first-person singular; the existence it affirms is that of an individual abstracted from the fundamental human condition of plurality. The world available to the thinking subject is a world available to being known from a unitary perspective. The world in which one feels shame, however, is one that is necessarily constituted by one's being-among-others and, as the very medium of one's relationship to a plurality of others, cannot be stabilized as an object of knowledge. If doubt is an epistemological problem, shame is a feature of ethical-political life that displaces for ethics and politics the governing authority of epistemology.

Only at night can Agee write of shame and then through the written record let it make its deferred appearance in the world. The writer reviews the memory of day at night. He does not reproduce the day's events chronologically but moves between four temporal planes:

> That of recall; of reception, contemplation, *in medias res*: for which I have set up this silence under darkness on this front porch as a sort of fore-stage to which from time to time the action may have occasion to return.
>
> "As it happened": the straight narrative at the prow as from the first to last day it cut unknown water.
>
> By recall and memory from the present: which is a part of the experience: and this includes imagination, which in the other planes I swear myself against.
>
> As I try to write it: problems of recording; which, too, are an organic part of the experience as a whole.
>
> These are, obviously, in strong conflict. So is any piece of human experience. So, then, inevitably, is any even partially accurate attempt to give any experience as a whole. (215)

For Agee, the " 'truest' thing about the experience is . . . as it turns up in recall . . . casting its lights and associations forward and backward," which operation gives the book its musical structure: "If this is so the book as a whole will have a form and set of tones rather less like those of narrative than like those of music" (215). Music is Agee's figure for the shuttling between temporal planes as well as genres, for the purpose of releasing to perceptibility the "truest" aspects of experience that are otherwise assimilated into the predictable order of day. Night affords release from what Agee calls "these daytime delusions": "We bask in our lavish little sun as children in the protective sphere of their parents: and perhaps can never outgrow, or can never dare afford to outgrow, our delusions of his strength and wisdom and of our intelligence, competence and safety; and we can carry over from him, like a green glow in the eyeballs, these daytime delusions . . ." (218) By day we habitually deny our fragility and vulnerability, which depends on the denial of the vulnerability of others, particularly, the father who traditionally figures as the paradigmatic source of authority. It is in his activity of nocturnal writing that Agee finds release from being governed by this diurnal illusion, an illusion that forms "the basis of our existence" and "is even simpler and even more literal than the need to eat and sleep" (219).

Readers may hear familiar echoes of Freud's theory of dreams in Agee's reflections on his procedures as a writer. The dreamer revisits at night the events of the day and, in processes of condensation, displacement, and abstraction, finds symbolic form for desires that cannot find expression in conscious speech. The work of analysis aims, then, to bring to consciousness such literally inexpressible desires and to open up through discursive transformation the subject's capacity for action. Agee indeed invokes Freud and psychoanalysis in his text, among a dense array of allusions to artists and thinkers, texts and disciplines of his cultural past and present. He resists, however, couching his authority in any one particular idiom, moving musically, rather, between heterogeneous idioms to generate effects of resonance. In his idiosyncratic way, Agee works during his nights of labor to bring to perceptibility what he literally could not say, had no language for, but that was nevertheless deeply part of his diurnal experience in Alabama in the summer of 1936. I have indicated that what Agee is trying to communicate is his experience of shame. But what is shame, and how does it manifest itself?

Shame, as I remarked earlier, is predicated on our existence as essentially plural human beings. In feeling shame, I feel shame in relation to another or others to whom I appear in a world *as* world among others. Shame has an ancient provenance. It played a major function in the ethical life of the ancient Greeks, but it has been by and large replaced in modern systems of morality by the regulatory notion of guilt. I cite a remarkable passage by the philosopher Bernard Williams, who sheds light in his book *Shame and Necessity* on the difference between shame and guilt and makes a case for the priority of the former.

Williams examines shame (*aidos*) in Greek epic and tragic literary texts to propose to us moderns certain "advantages in the Greeks' ways of understanding the ethical emotions."[25] "To the modern moral consciousness," Williams writes:

> guilt seems a more transparent emotion than shame. It may seem so, but that is only because, as it presents itself, it is more isolated than shame is from other elements of one's self-image, the rest of one's desires and needs, and because it leaves out a lot even of one's ethical consciousness. It can direct one towards those who have been wronged or damaged, and demand reparation in the name, simply, of what has happened to them. But it cannot by itself help one to understand one's relations to those happenings, or to rebuild the self that has done these things and the world in which that self has to live. Only shame can do that, because it embodies conceptions of what one is and of how one is related to others.[26]

In the "picture of the moral life" centered on guilt, Williams analyzes, "I am provided by reason, or perhaps by religious illumination . . . , with a knowledge of the moral law, and I need only the will to obey it. The structures most typical of shame then fall away: *what I am, so far as it affects the moral, is already given.*"[27] The self implicit in the "picture of moral life" centered on guilt is static, already given, as are the others with which this self lives. The self that feels shame in living with others is, in contrast, dynamic and capable of being shaped and reshaped in the experience of interaction with others, and of changing—or, to use Williams's term, "rebuilding"— itself and the very world in which it necessarily lives with others.

Agee attempts in his text to displace the dominant modern "picture of moral life" centered on guilt. He struggles to communicate his relationships with those he writes of not in terms strictly governed by guilt but as, more profoundly, structured by shame. His text has often been misread and belittled as "confessional" and "guilt-ridden." Such a reading insists on Agee's sense of responsibility for those he writes about as an insurmountable, inexpiable debt, and conceives of the relationship between Agee and the tenant farmers in hierarchical terms, predicated on a basis of inequality. There are various ways of describing this relationship: active/passive, empowered/disempowered; in economic terms, middle-class journalist versus subsistence-level sharecropper; in terms of educational level, intellectual versus illiterate or semiliterate. The conception of responsibility for the other as governed by guilt presupposes inequality as the basis of the relationship between subjects. According to this picture, who I am and who the other is are already given and not fundamentally at stake in the encounter. Agee seeks, through his writing, to move beyond the "daytime delusion" of this picture in which his authority would derive from and remain rooted in a predefined relationship of inequality.

He undertakes the task of writing himself out of this relationship and the world outside this picture, revisiting in his nights of writing diurnal scenes that had taken place in the summer of 1936. In these re-visitations, he analyzes and reveals to the reader what he did not or could not dwell on at the moment the incidents occurred.

One scene is narrated in an early section of the text titled "Near a Church." Agee and Evans had recently arrived in the area and were trying to gain access into an African American church they had stopped to photograph. A young couple walked by. Seeing them made Agee feel "ashamed and insecure in our wish to break into and possess their church, and after a minute or two I decided to go after them and speak to them, and ask them if they knew where we might find a minister or some other person who might let us in, if it would be all right" (36–7). When Agee got close to them, the girl started running. Agee realized the misunderstanding he had occasioned. He recounts apologizing for scaring them and the perfunctory exchange of "faked casualness" they then had about finding a way into the church. He threads this narration with the fantasy of throwing himself on the ground to "embrace and kiss their feet," which he dismissed as, at the least, more confusing than what had already taken place.

What is Agee trying to show in this passage? He exposes to the reader what he and the couple did not expose to each other, maintaining instead a facade of faked casualness that screened their respective sense of embarrassment and mutual loss of power. Agee recalls feeling ashamed of being seen by them as trespasser, then of being perceived as bigot or aggressor, and finally of mollifying them with his faked casualness. (Presumably he felt also embarrassment in perceiving the fear and embarrassment they exposed in misunderstanding why he followed them.) Neither party was in control of how they were perceived *by* the other, in possession of their image of themselves, and betrayed this incapacity to the other in their acting in misperception of the other. Precisely in betraying this incapacity—in shame—Agee discloses an aspect of who he is in relation to others with whom the disclosure is necessarily implicated. He makes the reader retroactively witness to this event.

A second scene occurs towards the end of the text but early in the chronology of the authors' visit to Alabama. In one of the last sections of the book, ironically titled "Inductions," Agee recounts his and Evans's initial encounter with one of the three families they would stay with, an encounter that would single out these human beings and not any others as the ones they would create their record about. Upon leaving the Ricketts house, without "any particular reason to think we would see either of you or any of these others," Agee remembers seeing "the unforgiving face, the eyes, of Mrs. Ricketts at her door: which has since stayed as a torn wound and sickness at the center of my chest, and perhaps more than any other thing has insured what I do not yet know: that we shall have to return, even in the face of causing further pain, until that mutual wounding shall have been won and healed, until she shall fear us no further, yet not in forgetfulness, but through ultimate trust, through love" (327).

What do Sadie Ricketts's distrustful eyes show Agee? They show him her pain. She discloses herself to him as one in pain, singularizing him as its addressee, and opening up in him a wound whose cause he does not understand but that has the power to move him into responsiveness. This discovery of a wound between Sadie Ricketts and himself occasions Agee's return to these three related families not just during July and August of 1936 but in the years of writing to follow. It initiates the writer's attempt creatively to reconstitute the self and the world in which that self has to live as actor and spectator, in which the disclosure of the self is radically—and shamefully—conditioned by exposure to others.

Let Us Now Praise Famous Men moves from the experience of shame to the possibility of praise. Praise is what the book in its rather unwieldy title proposes to do. "Let us now praise famous men" is the first verse of Ecclesiasticus 44, the first fourteen verses of which Agee inserts without any commentary toward the end of his text. The book declares its own incompleteness: according to Agee, is "merely portent and fragment, experiment, dissonant prologue" (xi), the first of a larger work titled *Three Tenant Families* that was never completed. In this light, praise is what this avowedly unfinished work does not accomplish but rather proleptically and interminably moves toward, seeks to create the conditions for. "Let" is a curious verb that—apart from transitively denoting what a landowner does—functions as a modal subjunctive and connotes a passivity that precedes activity.[28] "Let" clears the way for a "praise" that is not but is to come, a "praise" from an "us" that the text would create in its address as speakers of praise—and with that creation, "praise" can take place "now."

But what is praise? When I praise, I do not report or describe a verifiable proposition but perform a speech act. Yet praise is not, strictly speaking, an illocutionary performative utterance that names what it does, as in J. L. Austin's classic examples of "I promise, bet, wed, give, bequeath," that achieve their effect *in* saying something.[29] For such an illocutionary utterance to be successful or felicitous, it must adhere to an accepted conventional procedure having a certain conventional effect: for example, to accomplish the act of christening a ship, I must participate in a culture in which christening exists and be the one authorized to do the naming in the presence of the appropriate authorities in the appropriate place and time.

Praise does not strictly name what it accomplishes; as a perlocutionary utterance, it does *by* saying something and is closer to such instances as "I deter, punish, alarm, disgust, or seduce." In his extension or unfolding of Austin's categories, Stanley Cavell calls the latter "passionate utterances," expressive speech acts whose felicity cannot be evaluated according to conformity with accepted convention or procedure. The "I" that is moved to speak and demands a response in kind from "you" is not backed by affiliation with an institution or group: it is a singular "I" that singularizes a "you" with whom I declare myself to have standing. "A performative utterance," Cavell distinguishes, "is an offer of participation in the order of law. A passionate utterance is an invitation to improvisation in the disorders of desire."[30] In passionate utterance, the "I" calls on "you" to participate in an unlegislated event in which the future of our relationship is radically at stake.

In its movement toward the possibility of praise, *Let Us Now Praise Famous Men* moves musically toward the improvisation of a language for "us" that is in excess of established convention or procedure. It creates the conditions for a praise that demands for its success or felicity a response in kind from *you*, the reader. What is at stake is *our* future.

Notes

Introduction

1. See Stanley Cavell, *Disowning Knowledge in Six Plays of Shakespeare* (Cambridge: Cambridge University Press, 1976); and Harold Bloom, *Shakespeare: The Invention of the Human* (New York: Riverhead, 1998). Among recent books that consider Shakespeare's relationship to philosophy, see Colin McGinn, *Shakespeare's Philosophy: Discovering the Meaning behind the Plays* (New York: HarperCollins, 2006); and A. D. Nuttall, *Shakespeare the Thinker* (New Haven, CT: Yale University Press, 2007). For a recent treatment of Shakespeare's literary political legacy, see Linda Charnes, *Hamlet's Heirs: Shakespeare and the Politics of a New Millennium* (New York: Routledge, 2006).

2. Cf. Jacques Derrida, "La bête et le souverain," in *La démocratie à venir: Autour de Jacques Derrida*, ed. M.-L. Mallet (Paris: Galilée, 2004), 433–76; Derrida, *Voyous: Deux essais sur la raison* (Paris: Galilée, 2003); Derrida, *Without Alibi*, trans. Peggy Kamuf (Stanford, CA: Stanford University Press, 2002); and Giorgio Agamben, *Homo Sacer: Sovereign Power and Bare Life*, trans. Daniel Heller-Roazen (Stanford, CA: Stanford University Press, 1998).

3. See Carl Schmitt, *Political Theology: Four Chapters on the Concept of Sovereignty*, ed. and trans. George Schwab (Chicago: University of Chicago Press, 2005); Michel Foucault, *Security, Territory, Population: Lectures at the Collège de France, 1977–1978*, ed. Michel Senellart and trans. Graham Burchell (New York: Picador, 2007); and Foucault, *The Birth of Biopolitics: Lectures at the Collège de France, 1978–1979*, ed. Michel Senellart and trans. Graham Burchell (New York: Picador, 2008).

4. See Harold Bloom, *The Anxiety of Influence: A Theory of Poetry*, 2nd ed. (New York: Oxford University Press, 1997).

5. See James Chandler's *Wordsworth's Second Nature* (Chicago: University of Chicago Press, 1984) for his account of a Wordsworthian shift from Rousseau to Burke.

6. Arendt's phenomenological rethinking of politics and critique of the tradition of political philosophical is recently undergoing, more than thirty years after her death, a major critical revival. I have learned greatly from her work and cite her passim in the chapters to follow.

1. Sovereignty, Exposure, Theater: A Reading of King Lear

1. See R. A. Foakes's "Introduction" to his Arden edition of *King Lear* (London: Thomson Learning, 1997), 12–3; and Frank Kermode's "Introduction" to *King Lear* in *The Riverside Shakespeare*, ed. G. Blakemore Evans (Boston: Houghton Mifflin, 1974), 1249–51.

2. Cf. Leah Marcus's consideration of the timing of this performance in the context of James's relationship to Parliament in *Puzzling Shakespeare* (Berkeley and Los Angeles: University of California Press, 1988), 148–60.

3. Tim Spiekerman offers a lucidly provocative account in *Shakespeare's Political Realism: The English History Plays* (Albany: State University of New York Press, 2001) of how Shakespeare explores the question of legitimacy in selected histories that engage in complex conversation with Machiavellian realism.

4. The question of the text's instability is the center of Gary Taylor and Michael Warren's edited collection of essays, *The Division of the Kingdoms: Shakespeare's Two Versions of King Lear* (Oxford: Oxford University Press, 1983). I thank Margaret Maurer for showing me the tricky contours of the play's textual history.

5. The poet and Shakespeare scholar John Berryman formulates the problem and its stakes this way: "It will be well if the reader can discard from the outset the notion that there is in existence *a* text of *King Lear* which we shall be discussing. There was once, certainly, such a text, but it is lost. All we have are two widely different texts, a quarto of 1608 and the folio of 1623, as witnesses to it. They report, with upward of 1,200 serious variations, an event—Shakespeare's manuscript—which both of them have witnessed (at whatever remove) and we have not; what we have to do is to weigh their testimony, in order to reconstruct in its light the lost and important event of 1605–6." "Textual Introduction," in *Berryman's Shakespeare*, ed. John Haffenden (New York: Farrar, Straus & Giroux, 1999), 179. I thank Bruce Smith for bringing to my attention Berryman's Shakespeare scholarship.

6. All references to the text of *King Lear* in this essay will rely on the Arden version edited by R. A. Foakes that I cite above.

7. Quotation from "Notes on the Plays (1765, 1778)," in John Wain, ed., *Johnson as Critic* (London: Routledge and Kegan Paul, 1973), 217.

8. See "The Reception of *King Lear*" in Foakes's *Hamlet versus Lear: Cultural Politics and Shakespeare's Art* (Cambridge: Cambridge University Press, 1993). My thanks go to Susan Cerasano for referring me to Foakes's work.

9. "The Avoidance of Love" appeared first as the concluding essay in Cavell's *Must We Mean What We Say?* (New York: Scribner, 1969). It was then reprinted as the first essay after the introduction in his *Disowning Knowledge in Six Plays of Shakespeare* (Cambridge: Cambridge University Press, 1976).

10. Cavell, "Avoidance of Love," in *Disowning*, 46. Cavell refers to Paul Alpers's important essay "*King Lear* and the Theory of the Sight Pattern," in *In Defense of Reading*, ed. R. Brower and R. Poirier (New York: Dutton, 1963), 133–52.

11. Cavell, "Avoidance of Love," 57–8.

12. *Poetics*, 11.1452a30, *The Basic Works of Aristotle*, ed. Richard McKeon, trans. Ingram Bywater (New York: Random House, 1941).

13. *A Grammar of Motives* (Berkeley and Los Angeles: University of California Press, 1969), 23. As Burke explains, "[Substance] in its etymological origins would refer to an attribute of the thing's *context*, since that which supports or underlies a thing would be part of the thing's context. And a thing's context, being outside or beyond the thing, would be something that the thing is *not*" (23).

14. "*King Lear*: Its Form and Psychosis," in *Kenneth Burke on Shakespeare*, ed. Scott L. Newstok (West Lafayette, IN: Parlor Press, 2007), 158.

15. *The Seminar of Jacques Lacan*, book 7, *The Ethics of Psychoanalysis, 1959–1960*, ed. Jacques-Alain Miller, trans. Dennis Porter (New York: Norton, 1992), 305–10.

16. Cf. Emily Wilson's examination of the affinities between Oedipus's and Lear's situations in *Mocked with Death: Tragic Overliving from Sophocles to Milton* (Baltimore, MD: Johns Hopkins University Press, 2004).

17. Sophocles, *Oedipus at Colonus*, trans. Robert Fagles, in *The Theban Plays* (New York: Penguin, 1984), lines 430–1.

18. I am grateful to Irad Kimhi for helping me arrive at this formulation.

19. Lacan, *Ethics of Psychoanalysis*, 305.

20. Kenneth Burke, writing in 1969, sees in this situation a similarity with Florida, which is "a-swarm with oldsters who have willy-nilly abdicated from some office or other." "*King Lear*," 158.

21. I am indebted to Shoshana Felman's groundbreaking analysis of the "speaking power" of silence in a juridical context in her essay on the writer K-Zetnik's surprising collapse on the witness stand in the 1961 trial of Adolf Eichmann in Jerusalem. Borrowing Walter Benjamin's concept of "the expressionless" (*das Ausdruckslose*), Felman argues that "K-Zetnik's collapse can be defined as 'the caesura' of the trial: a moment of petrification that interrupts and ruptures the articulations of the law, and yet that grounds them by shattering their false totality into 'a fragment of the true world.' " "A Ghost in the House of Justice: Death and the Language of the Law," in *The Juridical Unconscious: Trials and Traumas in the Twentieth Century* (Cambridge, MA: Harvard University Press, 2002), 163–4.

22. See Giorgio Agamben's remarks on "whatever" as translation of the adjective "quodlibet" in the Scholastic enumeration of transcendentals, and his argument for rethinking community from the point of departure of "whatever singularities," in *The Coming Community*, trans. Michael Hardt (Minneapolis: University of Minnesota Press, 1993), 1–2.

23. In making this distinction, I have learned from Hannah Arendt's analysis of a Platonic legacy of thinking of freedom as end for which human communal life in the polis is organized as means, and—in tension with this prevalent Platonic tradition—the Kantian notion of freedom that is "associated with action and speech insofar as speech is an act," and that is "based on the ability of every human being to initiate a sequence, to forge a new chain." Arendt, "Introduction *into* Politics," in *The Promise of Politics*, ed. Jerome Kohn (New York: Schocken, 2005), 126.

24. Cf. political theorist Ernesto Laclau's discussion of the function of "zero" in Pascal's theory of numbers: "The zero is nothing, but it is the nothing of the system itself, the impossibility of its consistent closure, which is signified by the zero and in

that sense, paradoxically, the zero as empty place becomes the signifier of fullness, of systematicity as such, as that which is lacking." "The Politics of Rhetoric," in *Material Events: Paul de Man and the Afterlife of Theory*, ed. Tom Cohen, Barbara Cohen, J. Hillis Miller, and Andrzej Warminski (Minneapolis: University of Minnesota Press, 2001), 233. I thank Brian McGrath for pointing this passage out to me.

25. John F. Danby examines the two versions of "nature" invoked in the play in terms of the tension between a medieval vision of society and that of nascent capitalism in "The Two Natures and the Fission of Elizabethan Society," in *Shakespeare's Doctrine of Nature: A Study of King Lear* (London: Faber and Faber, 1951), 43–53. Danby writes, "For the two Natures and two Reasons imply two societies. Edmund belongs to the new age of scientific inquiry and industrial development, of bureaucratic organization and social regimentation, the age of mining and merchant-venturing, of monopoly and Empire-making, the age of the sixteenth century and after: an age of competition, suspicion, and glory" (46).

26. What Edmund wants is precisely to become a legitimate member of the kingdom, to have a title and part, and he wants to be recognized by others as a man with title and part. But Edmund is on a quest not just for legitimacy and power, but also for love. He mistakes, right until the end, being recognized as a man with a title and part in the kingdom for being loved. By instigating his plot, he lays claim to Edgar's land and thereby to his "father's love." He tries to convert himself into an object worthy of love. Cutting his own arm to feign an injury dealt by Edgar, he desperately cries, "Father, father!/Stop, stop, no help?" (2.1.36–7). Pathetically, he views himself confirmed as an object of love when, at the end of the play, he sees the dead bodies of Goneril and Regan and remarks, "Yet Edmund was beloved" (5.2.237).

27. Harold Bloom observes that "the play's central consciousness perforce is Edgar's, who actually speaks more lines than anyone except Lear." *Shakespeare: The Invention of the Human* (New York: Riverhead, 1998), 482.

28. I have learned from Alex Woloch's incisive analysis of the changing relationships between Lear and servant figures in the section "Interiority and Centrality in *Le Père Goriot* and *King Lear*," in *The One vs. the Many: Minor Characters and the Space of the Protagonist in the Novel* (Princeton, NJ: Princeton University Press, 2003), 288–95.

29. "The Tragic Substance," in Haffenden, *Berryman's Shakespeare*, 132.

30. Northrop Frye formulates his influential term "green world" in *Anatomy of Criticism* (New York: Atheneum, 1970), 182–4.

31. *The Claim of Reason: Wittgenstein, Skepticism, Morality, and Tragedy* (Oxford: Oxford University Press, 1979), 437.

32. Cited by Ernst Kantorowicz in *The King's Two Bodies: A Study in Medieval Political Theology* (Princeton, NJ: Princeton University Press, 1997), 7. Kantorowicz's source is Edmund Plowden's *Commentaries or Reports* (London, 1816), 212a.

33. Agamben makes his influential argument concerning "bare life" as the fundamental element of the political-theological tradition of the West, persisting even in modernity, most famously in *Homo Sacer: Sovereign Power and Bare Life*, trans.

Daniel Heller-Roazen (Stanford, CA: Stanford University Press, 1998). See also Agamben, *State of Exception*, trans Kevin Attell (Chicago: University of Chicago Press, 2005).

34. Aristotle, *Politics*, in McKeon, *Basic Works*, trans. Benjamin Jowett, 1253a9–10.

35. I have learned immensely from Hannah Arendt's phenomenology of politics in *The Human Condition*, 2nd ed. (Chicago: University of Chicago Press, 1998) and refer here to ideas expressed passim throughout the book.

36. Agamben, *Homo Sacer*, 8.

37. *A Voice and Nothing More* (Cambridge, MA: MIT Press, 2006), 106.

38. Arendt, *Human Condition*, 234.

39. Foakes reproduces this title page on p. 112 of his introduction to the Arden *King Lear*.

40. *The Life of the Mind* (San Diego: Harcourt Brace Jovanovich, 1978), 19.

41. In the recent critical literature on the affect of shame, I have found particularly instructive Joan Copjec's essay "May '68, The Emotional Month," which, examining Jacques Lacan's plea to the revolting university students for a display of shame, subtly distinguishes between shame and guilt as contrasting expressions of anxiety. The former is more radical, and the latter a hasty transformation of anxiety into "something knowable, possessable as an identity, a property, a surplus-value attaching to one's person." In *Lacan: The Silent Partners*, ed. Slavoj Zizek (London: Verso, 2006), 109.

42. Foakes cites Gerard in his footnote in the Arden *King Lear*, 344. The quote derives from John Gerard, *The Herball* (London: John Norton, 1597), 540.

43. "Words and Wounds," reprinted in *The Geoffrey Hartman Reader*, ed. Geoffrey Hartman and Daniel T. O'Hara (New York: Fordham University Press, 2004), 284.

44. Benedick tells Don Pedro and Claudio that, if he should ever fall in love, "pick out mine eyes with a ballad-maker's pen,/and hang me up at the door of a brothel-house for the sign of blind Cupid" (1.1.252–4). *Much Ado about Nothing* in Evans, *Riverside Shakespeare*.

45. Cf. Julia Reinhard Lupton and Kenneth Reinhard's inspired reading of this scene in *After Oedipus: Shakespeare in Psychoanalysis* (Ithaca, NY: Cornell University Press, 1993), 224.

46. Cf. Terence Cave's classic study of recognition scenes as bringing to the surface "all the possibilities that threaten wholeness" despite their claims to "resolve, conjoin and make whole." *Recognitions: A Study in Poetics* (Oxford: Clarendon Press, 1988), 489.

47. Among treatments of this topic, I have found particularly useful Janet Adelman's *Suffocating Mothers: Fantasies of Maternal Origin in Shakespeare's Plays, Hamlet to the Tempest* (New York: Routledge, 1991); and Coppélia Kahn's "The Absent Mother in *King Lear*," in *Rewriting the Renaissance: The Discourses of Sexual Difference in Early Modern Europe*, ed. Margaret W. Ferguson, Maureen Quilligan, and Nancy J. Vickers (Chicago: University of Chicago Press, 1986), 33–49.

48. Cf. Arendt on the power of forgiveness in *The Human Condition*, 236–43.

49. Jonathan Goldberg, "Perspectives: Dover Cliff and the Conditions of Representation," in *Shakespeare's Hand* (Minneapolis: University of Minnesota Press, 2003), 132–48; and Christopher Pye, "Vanishing Point," in *The Vanishing: Shakespeare, the Subject, and Early Modern Culture* (Durham, NC: Duke University Press, 2000), 65–104.

50. Cf. Jacques Lacan's classic discussion of the anamorphic decentering of the Cartesian subject of consciousness and vision in *The Seminar of Jacques Lacan*, book 11, *The Four Fundamental Concepts of Psycho-analysis*, ed. Jacques-Alain Miller, trans. Alan Sheridan (New York: Norton, 1981), 79–90.

51. "An End to Masterpieces," in *Antonin Artaud: Selected Writings*, ed. Susan Sontag, trans. Helen Weaver (Berkeley and Los Angeles: University of California Press, 1988), 254.

52. Cf. Joseph Wittreich, *Image of That Horror: History, Prophecy, and the Apocalypse in King Lear* (San Marino, CA: Huntington Library Press, 1984).

53. E. R. Curtius comments magisterially on this metaphor in *European Literature and the Latin Middle Ages*, trans. Willard Trask (Princeton, NJ: Princeton University Press, 1973), 138–44.

54. *As You Like It*, 2.7.139–40, in Evans, *Riverside Shakespeare*.

2. Wordsworth on the Heath: Tragedy, Autobiography, and the Revolutionary Spectator

1. Jonathan Bate discusses the question of Wordsworth's debt to Shakespeare in chapters 4 and 5 of *Shakespeare and the English Romantic Imagination* (Oxford: Clarendon Press, 1986).

2. Keats coins the famous phrase and contrasts Wordsworth with Shakespeare in his letter to Richard Woodhouse of October 27, 1818. *Letters of John Keats*, ed. Robert Gittings (Oxford: Oxford University Press, 1970), 157–8.

3. See Juliet Barker's account of the contemporaneous literary efforts of these Romantic poets in chapters 6 and 7 of *Wordsworth: A Life* (New York: Ecco, 2005), 101–44. See also Kenneth Johnston's biography of the young Wordsworth in *William Wordsworth: Poet, Lover, Rebel, Spy* (New York: Norton, 1998); and Nicholas Roe's *Wordsworth and Coleridge: The Radical Years* (Oxford: Clarendon Press, 1988).

4. "The Fenwick Note (1843)" in the Cornell Wordsworth Edition of *The Borderers*, ed. Robert Osborn (Ithaca, NY: Cornell University Press, 1982), 814. All future references to this text will be documented in the body of the chapter. In the case of prefatory or postfatory material, citation of page number will follow "Preface," "1842 Note," or "Fenwick Note." I will be citing from the 1797–9 version of the play.

5. Mortimer and Rivers's names are changed to Marmaduke and Oswald, and Matilda's to Idonea in the 1842 revision.

6. See Johnston, *William Wordsworth*; Mary Moorman, *William Wordsworth: The Early Years* (Oxford: Oxford University Press, 1957); David Erdman, "Wordsworth as Heartsworth; or, Was Regicide the Prophetic Ground of Those 'Moral Questions'?" in *The Evidence of the Imagination: Studies of Interactions between Life and Art in*

English Romantic Literature, ed. Donald Reiman, Michael Jaye, and Betty Bennet (New York: New York University Press, 1978), 12–41; Mary Jacobus, " 'That Great Stage Where Senators Perform': Macbeth and the Politics of Romantic Theatre," in *Romanticism, Writing, and Sexual Difference* (Oxford: Clarendon Press, 1989), 33–68; and David Bromwich, "Political Justice and *The Borderers*," in *Disowned by Memory: Wordsworth's Poetry of the 1790s* (Chicago: University of Chicago Press, 1998) 44–68.

7. Jean-Jacques Rousseau, *The Confessions*, trans. J. M. Cohen (London: Penguin, 1953), 17.

8. *The Human Condition*, 2nd ed. (Chicago: University of Chicago Press, 1998), 178–81.

9. Ibid., 177.

10. Ibid., 181.

11. Ibid., 184.

12. I am indebted to Parker's illuminating readings of the play in " 'Oh Could You Hear His Voice!': Wordsworth, Coleridge, and Ventriloquism," in *Romanticism and Language*, ed. Arden Reed (Ithaca, NY: Cornell University Press, 1984), 125–43; "Reading Wordsworth's Power: Narrative and Usurpation in *The Borderers*," *ELH* 54 (1987): 299–331; and " 'In Some Sort Seeing with My Proper Eyes': Wordsworth and the Spectacles of Paris," *Studies in Romanticism* 27 (1988): 369–90. This latter issue of *Studies in Romanticism* is devoted to *The Borderers* and contains also excellent essays by William Jewett, "Action in *The Borderers*" (399–400); and David Marshall, "The Eyewitnesses of *The Borderers*" (391–8).

13. Parker, "Reading Wordsworth's Power," 306.

14. Ibid., 308.

15. Hazlitt quotes this speech in an 1819 lecture on the novels of Godwin "to illustrate the necessitarian theory of action" (Bromwich, "Political Justice and *The Borderers*," 45). And Coleridge quotes these lines in his lecture on *Hamlet* in his 1813 series of lectures on Shakespeare, according to Jonathan Bate, "Introduction," in *The Romantics on Shakespeare*, ed. Jonathan Bate (London: Penguin, 1997), 21.

16. See Stefanie Markovits's reading of *The Borderers* as an investigation of the relationship between action and consciousness in "Wordsworth's Revolution: From *The Borders* to *The White Doe of Rylstone*," in *The Crisis of Action in Nineteenth-Century English Literature* (Columbus: Ohio State University Press, 2006), 11–46.

17. Scholars have researched how Wordsworth was likely to have crafted aspects of the Rivers-Captain relationship after the relationship between Caleb Williams and Falkland in Godwin's novel *Caleb Williams*, and to have used as a significant source the historical trial of the mutineers against the captain of the HMS *Bounty* in 1793–4. See Geoffrey Sanborn, "The Madness of Mutiny: Wordsworth, the *Bounty*, and *The Borderers*," *Wordsworth Circle* 23 (1992): 35–42; Marjean D. Purinton, "Wordsworth's *The Borderers* and the Ideology of Revolution," *Wordsworth Circle* 23 (1992): 97–108; and Victoria Myers, "Justice and Indeterminacy: Wordsworth's *The Borders* and the Trials of the 1790s," *Studies in Romanticism* 40 (2001): 427–57.

18. Walter Benjamin writes memorably in his essay "The Storyteller: Reflections on the Works of Nikolai Leskov": "It is . . . characteristic that not only a man's knowledge or wisdom, but above all his real life—and this is the stuff that stories are made of—first assumes transmissible form at the moment of his death. Just as a sequence of images is set in motion inside a man as his life comes to an end—unfolding the views of himself under which he has encountered himself without being aware of it—suddenly in his expressions and looks the unforgettable emerges and imparts to everything that concerned him that authority which even the poorest wretch in dying possesses for the living around him. This authority is at the very source of the story." In *Illuminations*, ed. Hannah Arendt, trans. Harry Zohn (New York: Schocken, 1968), 94.

19. As a function designating an immemorial blind spot in Mortimer's memory and imagination, the heath looks forward (or backward, in terms of the chronology of Wordsworth's life) to the two definitive "spots of time" in *The Prelude*, already in the two-part version of 1799: in which Wordsworth recalls being separated from his guide as a child and seeing a gibbet-mast and, on another occasion, waiting on top of a hill for the horses that would bear him and his brother home. The numerous instances of heath-like landscapes in Wordsworth's oeuvre—*Salisbury Plain* offers one obvious example close in date of composition to *The Borderers*—deserve further scrutiny, and can be approached on several levels: on that of Wordsworth's work, of his biography, in terms of literary influence, or as part of his meditation on the formation of consciousness. My sense of the uncanniness of place in Wordsworth is indebted to Geoffrey Hartman's unparalleled attentiveness to the poet's subtly disquieting power in *Wordsworth's Poetry, 1787–1814* (New Haven, CT: Yale University Press, 1964); and *The Unremarkable Wordsworth* (Minneapolis: University of Minnesota Press, 1987).

3. Poetry against Indifference: Responding to "The Discharged Soldier"

1. These positions are represented by, among many others, David Bromwich, *Disowned by Memory: Wordsworth's Poetry of the 1790s* (Chicago: University of Chicago Press, 1998); James Chandler, *Wordsworth's Second Nature: A Study of the Poetry and Politics* (Chicago: University of Chicago Press, 1984); Gary Harrison, *Wordsworth's Vagrant Muse: Poetry, Poverty, and Power* (Detroit: Wayne State University Press, 1994); Marjorie Levinson, *Wordsworth's Great Period Poems* (New York: Cambridge University Press, 1986); and David Simpson, *Wordsworth's Historical Imagination: The Poetry of Displacement* (New York: Methuen, 1987). See also R. Clifton Spargo, "Begging the Question of Responsibility: The Vagrant Poor in Wordsworth's 'Beggars' and 'Resolution and Independence.'" *Studies in Romanticism* 39 (2000): 51–80.

2. Frederick Garber, *Wordsworth and the Poetry of Encounter* (Urbana: University of Illinois Press, 1971).

3. See Kenneth R. Johnston, "Wordsworth and *The Recluse*," in *The Cambridge Companion to Wordsworth*, ed. Stephen Gill (Cambridge: Cambridge University Press, 2003), 70–89.

4. Cf. Beth Darlington, "Two Early Texts: *A Night-Piece* and *The Discharged Soldier*," in *Bicentenary Wordsworth Studies: In Memory of John Alban Finch* (Ithaca, NY: Cornell University Press, 1970), 425–48.

5. All quotations from "The Discharged Soldier" and "The Old Cumberland Beggar" are from the Cornell Wordsworth Series edition of *Lyrical Ballads, and Other Poems, 1797–1800*, ed. James Butler and Karen Green (Ithaca, NY: Cornell University Press, 1992).

6. I have learned much from Paul Fry's readings of how Wordsworth's poetry opens up the possibility of experiencing the world as without particular qualification or significance. For a juxtaposition of Wordsworth with Heidegger, see "Clearings in the Way: Non-epiphany in Wordsworth," in *A Defense of Poetry: Reflections on the Occasion of Writing* (Stanford, CA: Stanford University Press, 1995), 91–107; on Wordsworth's importance for ecological thought, "Green to the Very Door? The Natural Wordsworth," in *The Wordsworthian Enlightenment: Romantic Poetry and the Ecology of Reading*, ed. Helen Elam and Frances Ferguson (Baltimore, MD: Johns Hopkins University Press, 2005), 97–111. See also his recent collection of essays on Wordsworth, *Wordsworth and the Poetry of What We Are* (New Haven, CT: Yale University Press, 2008).

7. All quotations from *The Prelude* are from the Norton Critical Edition of *The Prelude: 1799, 1805, 1850*, ed. Jonathan Wordsworth, M. H. Abrams, and Stephen Gill (New York: Norton, 1979).

8. 8 Cf. Lamentations 1:12: "*Is it* nothing to you, all ye that pass by? behold, and see if there be any sorrow like unto my sorrow, which is done unto me, wherewith the LORD hath afflicted *me* in the day of his fierce anger." *The Bible: Authorized King James Version*, ed. Robert Carroll and Stephen Prickett (Oxford: Oxford University Press, 1997).

9. Cf. *Paradise Lost*, 2.666–70: "The other shape / If shape it might be call'd that shape had none / Distinguishable in member, joynt, or limb, / Or substance might be call'd that shadow seem'd, / For each seem'd either. . . ." *The Riverside Milton*, ed. Roy Flannagan (Boston: Houghton Mifflin, 1998).

10. Hannah Arendt, *The Human Condition*, 2nd ed. (Chicago: University of Chicago Press, 1998), 7–8.

11. Hannah Arendt, *The Life of the Mind* (San Diego: Harcourt Brace Jovanovich, 1978).

12. *Wordsworth and the Enlightenment: Nature, Man, and Society in the Experimental Poetry* (New Haven, CT: Yale University Press, 1989), 84.

13. Nancy Yousef describes Wordsworth's "cowardly withdrawal from the other" as "a minor act of ethical bad faith" in "Wordsworth, Sentimentalism, and the Defiance of Sympathy," *European Romantic Review* 17 (2006): 211.

14. Friedrich Nietzsche, *On the Genealogy of Morals* and *Ecce Homo*, ed. and trans. Walter Kaufmann (New York: Vintage, 1967).

15. Cf. Jacques Rancière, *Disagreement: Politics and Philosophy*, trans. Julie Rose (Minneapolis: University of Minnesota Press, 1999). See Rancière's writings on

Wordsworth in *Short Voyages to the Land of the People*, trans. James B. Swenson (Stanford, CA: Stanford University Press, 2003); and *The Flesh of Words: The Politics of Writing*, trans. Charlotte Mandell (Stanford, CA: Stanford University Press, 2004).

16. See Shoshana Felman's development of Walter Benjamin's concept of *das Ausdruckslose* or "the expressionless" in *The Juridical Unconscious: Trials and Traumas in the Twentieth Century* (Cambridge, MA: Harvard University Press, 2002).

17. Giorgio Agamben, *Homo Sacer: Sovereign Power and Bare Life*, trans. Daniel Heller-Roazen (Stanford, CA: Stanford University Press, 1998).

4. From the Division of Labor to the Discovery of the Common: James Agee and Walker Evans's Let Us Now Praise Famous Men

1. James Agee and Walker Evans, *Let Us Now Praise Famous Men* (1941; repr., Boston: Houghton Mifflin, 2001), x. All further references to this edition of the text will be indicated by page number within the body of the chapter.

2. Evans's photographs were widely praised, but Agee's prose generated mixed responses, none of them dispassionate. The reviewer for *Time* called it "the most distinguished failure of the season." *Time*, October 13, 1941, 104. Lionel Trilling proclaimed it in the *Kenyon Review* "the most realistic and the most important moral effort of our American generation." *Kenyon Review* 4 (1942): 102. L. R. Etzkorn found parts of the text "almost the ravings of a lunatic." *Library Journal* 66 (1941): 667. And J. C. Cort found "the book . . . too repetitious, too obscure, too obsessed with irrelevant detail, and particularly too obsessed with the author's complex reactions to his subject and to everything else from Cézanne to Kafka [and] his own relatives." *Commonweal* 34 (1941): 499.

3. In his introduction to the 1988 edition of *Let Us Now Praise Famous Men*, the journalist and friend of the authors John Hersey recalls being surrounded in the summer of 1964 in Holmes County, Mississippi, by "northern white college kids who had risked their lives—and those of their black hosts—by invading the state that summer to help with voter registration. An astonishing number of them had brought Agee along with them. They gave his book to the young blacks of the Student Nonviolent Coordinating Committee." "Introduction: Agee," in *Let Us Now Praise Famous Men* (1960; repr., Boston: Houghton Mifflin, 1988), xxxvii. Another eyewitness, the psychiatrist Robert Coles, remembers "finding copies of the book . . . all over the South, especially in Freedom Houses, as we called them back in the summer of 1964 during the voter-registration projects in the steadfastly segregationist Delta." *James Agee: His Life Remembered* (New York: Holt, Rinehart and Winston, 1985), 97.

4. Agee calls his ersatz table of contents "Design of Book Two" in the 1941 edition. For the 1960 edition, this designation was changed to "Design of the Book." It may also be the case that Agee uses the designation of "Book Two" to indicate the book's place within the anticipated but unwritten trilogy.

5. I quote from *Republic*, 2.369d, *The Collected Dialogues of Plato*, ed. Edith Hamilton and Huntington Cairns (Princeton, NJ: Princeton University Press, 1989), 616. Paul Shorey is the translator of the *Republic* for this edition.

6. Henry Luce's publishing empire included *Time* (founded in 1923), *Fortune* (founded 1930), and *Life* (1936). He would found in the 1950s *House and Home* and *Sports Illustrated*. Time Inc. is, of course, now part of Time Warner Inc.

7. Jacques Rancière, *The Politics of Aesthetics*, trans. Gabriel Rockhill (London: Continuum, 2004), 12–3.

8. Jacques Rancière, "Introducing Disagreement," trans. Steven Corcoran, *Angelaki* 9 (2004): 6.

9. Ibid.

10. In the idiom of Jean-Luc Nancy, whose thinking of politics bears close comparison with that of Rancière, Agee and Evans could be said to perform an "unworking" (*désoeuvrement*). "Community cannot arise from the domain of *work*. . . . Community understood as a work or through its works would presuppose that the common being, as such, be objectifiable and producible (in sites, persons, buildings, discourses, institutions, symbols: in short, in subjects). . . . Community necessarily takes place in what Blanchot has called 'unworking,' referring to that which, before or beyond the work, withdraws from the work, and which, no longer having to do either with production or with completion, encounters interruption, fragmentation, suspension. . . . Communication is the unworking of work that is social, economic, technical, and institutional." *The Inoperative Community*, ed. Peter Connor (Minneapolis: University of Minnesota Press, 1991), 31.

11. Janis Bergman-Carton and Evan Carton, "James Agee, Walker Evans: Tenants in the House of Art." *Raritan* 20 (2001): 9.

12. Ibid.

13. Alan Trachtenberg writes, "It is clear from his record of publication that Evans characteristically thought of his pictures as comprising sequences, forming an order in and of themselves." *Reading American Photographs: Images as History, Matthew Brady to Walker Evans* (New York: Hill and Wang, 1989), 241.

14. Evans defined his distinctive style in contradistinction to art photography and commercial photography. About the art photographer, he writes in a 1931 essay: "The latter half of the nineteenth century offers that fantastic figure, the art photographer, really an unsuccessful painter with a bag of mysterious tricks. He is by no means a dead tradition even now, still gathered into clubs to exhibit pictures of misty October lanes, snow scenes, reflets dans l'eau, young girls with crystal balls." In "The Reappearance of Photography," in *Classic Essays on Photography*, ed. Alan Trachtenberg (New Haven, CT: Leete's Island Books, 1980), 185.

15. Ibid.

16. Leslie Katz, "Interview with Walker Evans," *Art in America* 59 (1971): 84.

17. Cf. Aristotle, *De anima*, book 2, chapter 11, in *The Basic Works of Aristotle*, ed. Richard McKeon, trans. J. A. Smith (New York: Random House, 1941).

18. Two excellent books on the "ocularcentric" discourse of Western thought are Martin Jay's *Downcast Eyes: The Denigration of Vision in Twentieth-Century French Thought* (Berkeley and Los Angeles: University of California Press, 1993); and David Michael Levin, ed., *Sites of Vision: The Discursive Construction of Sight in the History of Philosophy* (Cambridge, MA: MIT Press, 1997).

19. In his pathbreaking recent book *Becoming Visionary: Brian de Palma's Cinematic Education of the Senses* (Stanford, CA: Stanford University Press, 2007), Eyal Peretz studies cinema as an apparatus of sensation, evolving a new conceptual model of the relationship between the senses and of the logic of sense itself. Prefacing his deft readings of De Palma's films, Peretz provides an introduction useful to the general scholarly reader. See "Introduction: The Realm of the Senses and the Vision of the Beyond—Toward a New Thinking of the Image," pp. 1–21.

20. I do not include page numbers where they do not appear in the edition. The preface features page numbers in Roman numerals, but the rest of the prefatory material—the epigraphs, a list of "Persons and Places," the title page, the "Design of the Book," the "Dedicatory Verses to Evans"—appear on unnumbered pages.

21. The footnote reads as follows: "These words are quoted here to mislead those who will be misled by them. They mean, not what the reader may care to think they mean, but what they say. They are not dealt with directly in this volume; but it is essential that they be used here, for in the pattern of the work as a whole, they are, in the sonata form, the second theme; the poetry facing them is the first. In view of the average reader's tendency to label, and of topical dangers to which any man, whether honest, or intelligent, or subtle, is at present liable, it may be well to make the explicit statement that neither these words nor the authors are the property of any political party, faith, or faction."

22. On the persistence of night as a metaphor for art's unworking of the logic of the day, see Elisabeth Bronfen's *Tiefer als der Tag Gedacht: Eine Kulturgeschichte der Nacht* (Munich: Hanser, 2008), which surveys representations of the night in literature, art, film, philosophy, and psychoanalysis from ancient Greek mythology to Martin Scorsese.

23. René Descartes, *Meditations on First Philosophy*, 3rd ed., trans. Donald A. Cress (Indianapolis: Hackett, 1993), 14.

24. Ibid.

25. *Shame and Necessity* (Berkeley and Los Angeles: University of California Press, 1993), 92.

26. Ibid., 94.

27. Ibid., 94–5, emphasis mine.

28. I thank Deborah Knuth Klenck for edifying me that "let" is a modal subjunctive.

29. *How to Do Things with Words* (Cambridge, MA: Harvard University Press, 1975).

30. "Performative and Passionate Utterance," in *Philosophy the Day after Tomorrow* (Cambridge, MA: Harvard University Press, 2005), 185. See also in the same collection of essays, "Fred Astaire Asserts the Right to Praise," 61–82.

Index